GERMAN STRATEGY IN THE GREAT WAR

BY
BREVET LIEUT.-COLONEL
PHILIP NEAME
V.C., D.S.O., p.s.c., ROYAL ENGINEERS

The Naval & Military Press Ltd

Published by

The Naval & Military Press Ltd
Unit 5 Riverside, Brambleside
Bellbrook Industrial Estate
Uckfield, East Sussex
TN22 1QQ England

Tel: +44 (0)1825 749494

www.naval-military-press.com
www.nmarchive.com

In reprinting in facsimile from the original, any imperfections are inevitably reproduced and the quality may fall short of modern type and cartographic standards.

CONTENTS

CHAPTER I
INTRODUCTORY

	PAGE
Command in War	1
Transportation	2
Weapons of the Future	3
German High Command	3

CHAPTER II
THE GERMAN STRATEGIC PLAN

1871	6
Plan of 1873	6
Plan of 1879	6
Plan of 1891	7
Schlieffen's Final Plan	8
The Plan of 1914	10
The Plan in Detail	11
Observations Regarding the Plan	13

CHAPTER III
THE FRONTIER BATTLES ON THE WESTERN FRONT

The German Advance in the West	16
The Operations of the Sixth and Seventh German Armies	17
The Battle in Lorraine, 20th–23rd August	19
The Wheel through Belgium	20
The Attack on the Trouée de Charmes, 25th–27th August	22

CONTENTS

CHAPTER IV
THE CHANGE IN THE GERMAN PLAN OF CAMPAIGN

	PAGE
The Battle of Guise—St. Quentin, 29th–30th August	24
Kluck's South-East Wheel	26
German Offensive Against French Right Wing, 4th–8th September	28

CHAPTER V
BATTLE OF THE MARNE AND EVENTS IN THE WEST TO THE END OF 1914

The Battle of the Marne	31
The Hentsch Episode and the Retreat	32
Moltke as a Commander	33
Change in German Supreme Command	35
Observations on the Campaign	37
Railways	39
The Value of Fortresses	41
The Race to the Sea	42
First Battle of Ypres	42

CHAPTER VI
RUSSIAN PLAN OF CAMPAIGN

The Plan	44
Situation in the East	46

CHAPTER VII
BATTLES OF TANNENBERG AND THE MASURIAN LAKES

Tannenberg	49
Masurian Lakes	57

CHAPTER VIII
FIRST AND SECOND INVASIONS OF POLAND

First Invasion of Poland	61
The Russian Counter-Offensive	62
The Second Invasion of Poland	63
The Battle of Lodz	64
Russian Counter-Measures	65

CONTENTS

	PAGE
Characters of the Russian Commanders	66
Success by Fifth Russian Army	67
Failure of Rennenkampf and the "Lovich Force"	67
The General Situation End of 1914	69
Observations	69

CHAPTER IX
"1915"

Situation at the Beginning of 1915	72
Winter Battle in Masuria	73
Great Offensive in Russia, 1915	75
Defensive in the West	79
Campaign in Serbia	80
Observations	80

CHAPTER X
"1916"

Situation at the Beginning of 1916	81
Verdun	83
Russian Offensive, March, 1916	83
Brusilov's Offensive	84
Cavalry in Brusilov's Offensive	86
The Somme	87
Falkenhayn	89
Ludendorff and the Somme	90
Observations	91

CHAPTER XI
THE RUMANIAN CAMPAIGN

Observations	95

CHAPTER XII
"1917"

The *Entente* Offensive in the West, 1917	96
Russian Revolution	98
Defence in Flanders	98
The Italian Campaign	99
Cambrai	100
Observations	100

CONTENTS

CHAPTER XIII

PREPARATIONS FOR THE OFFENSIVE IN 1918

	PAGE
Decision to Attack in the West	101
Locality of the Attack	102
German Tactics in 1918	104

CHAPTER XIV

THE FIVE GERMAN OFFENSIVES IN 1918

The First Attack, Arras—La Fère	106
The Lys Battle	110
Situation at the End of April	111
Observations	112
Attack on the Chemin des Dames, 27th May	113
Attack at Noyon, 9th June	113
Plans for the Final Attacks at Rheims and in Flanders	113
Entente Counter-Stroke	114
Observations on the German Offensives	116

CHAPTER XV

LUDENDORFF

Ludendorff's Career	118
Ludendorff's Character	120

APPENDICES

APPENDIX I.	Normal German Organization in 1914	123
APPENDIX II.	Order of Battle of German Armies, August, 1914	125
APPENDIX III.	Order of Battle at the Battles of the Marne, Verdun, Nancy, 6th September, 1914	128
APPENDIX IV.	Russian Organization and Order of Battle, 1914	130
APPENDIX V.	List of Books Consulted	132

MAPS

		PAGE
I	Concentration Areas of German and *Entente* Armies	20
II	Schlieffen's Plan of Campaign.	22
III	German Advance up to 5th September	30
IV	O.H.L. Order of 28th August for Further Conduct of Campaign	30
V	Situation at the Crisis of the Marne, 8th–9th September	42
VI	The Race to the Sea, 1914	42
VII	Strategical Deployment in the East	48
VIII	Tannenberg	58
IX	Masurian Lakes	60
X	Second Invasion of Poland	70
XI	Battle of Lodz	70
XII	German Offensive in Russia, 1915	80
XIII	Rumanian Campaign	94
XIV	Russian Offensives in 1916 and 1917	98
XV	Entente Offensive, April, 1917	100
XVI	German Offensives in 1918	116
XVII	German Attack, 21st March, 1918	116

NOTE.—Place names are spelt in accordance with the international $\frac{1}{1,000,000}$ map, except in the case of well-known places, when the English spelling is given (e.g. WARSAW).

GERMAN STRATEGY IN THE GREAT WAR

CHAPTER I

INTRODUCTORY

SCOPE OF BOOK

This book is the result of the history studied and opinions expressed in a series of lectures given at the Staff College, Camberley, between 1920 and 1923.

No attempt has been made to give a connected narrative of all the German operations during the war. All that has been attempted is to discuss the more important crises which occurred, and their effect on the German high command and German strategy. The year 1914 has been dealt with more fully than succeeding years, for position warfare gave little scope to strategy. The book should be regarded as a framework on which to base more detailed study of the various campaigns.

COMMAND IN WAR

The most fascinating part has been the study of the personality of the commanders, and I would commend this question to all who wish to study war. Surely the most vital decision that a Government has to make on the outbreak of war, is the selection of the Commander-in-Chief. That decision may make or mar the army. All troops will fight well if led well.

Foch has written :—" Great results in war are due to the

2 GERMAN STRATEGY IN THE GREAT WAR

commander. History is therefore right in making generals responsible for victories—in which case they are glorified ; and for defeats—in which case they are disgraced. Without a commander, no battle, no victory is possible."

And, of course, Napoleon's words :—" The Gauls were not conquered by the Roman legions, but by Cæsar. It was not before the Carthaginian soldiers that Rome was made to tremble, but before Hannibal. It was not the Macedonian phalanx which penetrated to India, but Alexander. . . ."

Now if we turn to the opening phases of the Great War, we see that no nation had succeeded in solving the problem of the selection of its higher commanders, that is, the Commanders-in-Chief and Army Commanders. Within a year or two every original Commander-in-Chief had vanished. Moltke went within six weeks, a failure. Every German Army Commander, except royal princes, went within a few months, half the French and Russian Army Commanders were replaced.

TRANSPORTATION

Another of the great lessons of the war is the importance of " transportation " in all its branches for large armies.

It appears that the German high command realized this before the war to a far greater extent than either the British or French.

We have only to remember the great Moltke's dictum after his successful wars of 1866 and 1870 in which railways played an important part for the first time in history :—
" Build no more fortresses, build railways."

Again, Schlieffen wrote as follows :—" Railways are now an engine of war without which the great armies of the future can neither be formed, concentrated, deployed nor maintained. One no longer asks only for the number of the enemy's battalions, one asks also : what is the extent of his railways ? One compares not only the efficiency and equipment of his troops with our own, one also seeks accurate information as to the capacity of his railways."

INTRODUCTORY 3

It will be pointed out in the following pages how the proper use of railways influenced the early German operations on the eastern front, such as the battles of Tannenberg, Lodz, etc., and how better use might have been made of railway transport on the west during the battle of the Marne.

The crisis which arose in transportation on the British front in the west in 1916 will be remembered. The Germans, although they had their difficulties, maintained to the end of the war the transportation organization with which they started. This organization expanded to cope with all requirements as they arose.

WEAPONS OF THE FUTURE

It will be observed that little notice has been given in this book to the new weapons of war, air, gas and tanks. The book deals in the main with strategy. The German strategy was but little influenced by these weapons, although tanks undoubtedly had a very large effect on the Entente plans in 1918. Air and gas still rested principally in the realms of tactics only up to 1918, although our Independent Air Force was just beginning to exert a larger influence.

It must not be thought that these new ideas in warfare—air, gas, tanks and cross-country traction—will not in the near future sway the strategy of armies because they are only touched on lightly here.

In studying the lessons of the past, it is well also to look forward.

GERMAN HIGH COMMAND

Before discussing the strategical aspect of the war from the German point of view, it is necessary to have a clear idea of the organization and methods of the German High Command.

The Kaiser was the Supreme War Lord, that is, Commander-in-Chief of the Army and Navy. Theoretically he

4 GERMAN STRATEGY IN THE GREAT WAR

exercised his command through the Prussian Chief of the General Staff of the Army, and the German Chief of the Naval Staff for the Navy. In actual practice orders were issued by the Chief of Staff in the Kaiser's name, and the Chief of Staff was the actual Commander-in-Chief who merely procured the Kaiser's concurrence in any important decision.

In the beginning of the war the biggest formation in the German Army was the Army, and these armies, each consisting of a varying number of Army Corps, were directly under O.H.L. (Supreme Command). Owing to the formation of many new armies and the extension of fronts, armies were grouped together into several army groups; the first of these to be formed was that of the Commander-in-Chief in the East at the end of September, 1914. A month or so later the western front was divided into three army groups.

The German General Staff, which provided the trained staff for all formations from a division upwards, was divided into two distinct classes, the " Great General Staff " and the " General Staff with troops." The former provided the staff at Supreme Command, and with armies, at the beginning of the war, that is, the higher command. The latter provided the staffs of Army Corps and Divisions, and were regarded as staffs of fighting formations.

The Great General Staff were, therefore, the most powerful element in the army. In peace time they prepared all the plans for war, and in war they carried them out. Normally the actual personnel who worked at the War Office in peace on plans for mobilization, concentration and the initial operations formed the operations staff at Supreme Command on the outbreak of war.

It is noticeable that the commanders of most of the German army groups, more especially those on the Western Front which were in closest touch with Supreme Command, were princes or dukes who must have been in a large measure nominal commanders dependent on their Chief of

Staff. It is not until one gets down to the armies that one finds experienced fighting commanders. This arrangement tended to keep the higher control very much in the hands of the Staff Officers of the Great General Staff, and increased the influence of the Chief of the General Staff who was responsible for the appointment of all General Staff Officers, whilst the Kaiser's Military Cabinet appointed the Commanders.

It may, I think, be of value to compare very briefly the supreme direction of the war on the part of Germany and of this country. There is no question but that Germany had divided control, divided between Supreme Command on the military side, and the Imperial Chancellor and his Ministers on the civil side. Theoretically the Kaiser was the single controlling head. Actually there were continual differences arising between the successive Chiefs of the General Staff, Moltke, Falkenhayn and Ludendorff (or Hindenburg) and the Chancellors Bethmann Hollweg, Michaelis, Count Hertling, and Prince Max of Baden. Supreme Command had little or no direct power of moulding the civil structure of the country to warlike purposes. They were dependent on the Imperial Chancellor for this, and the latter appears to have failed at times to get the maximum military effort out of the country. The German constitution required a man like Bismarck for the machinery to run really efficiently. The Chancellor was not appointed by national will or wish, but by the personal whim of the Kaiser.

This is not the place to discuss any political aspect of the direction of the war in England, but at all events the Constitution provides for single and united direction by the Prime Minister, who depends for his office on the national will.

CHAPTER II
THE GERMAN STRATEGIC PLAN

1871

In 1871, after the Franco-Prussian War, the elder Moltke considered the German Army capable of carrying out an offensive campaign on both the French and Russian fronts in the event of a war with the two Powers. France was exhausted and Russia undeveloped as a fighting power.

PLAN OF 1873

By 1873 France's rapid recovery rendered this impossible, and at that time the plan involved an immediate attack on France and a defensive attitude against Russia.

During the next few years France rendered her eastern frontier from Belfort to Longwy almost impregnable to the armies and weapons of that day by means of a series of fortresses. In front line the Belfort—Epinal group in the south and the Toul—Verdun group in the north, with an intentional gap of 40 miles between, the Trouée de Charmes, which we shall see was used to good purpose by the French on the defensive in 1914.

Behind these lay the Besançon—Langres—Dijon triangle in the south, Rheims and Laon in the north. Still farther in rear were the fortified areas of Lyons and Paris. (Map II.)

PLAN OF 1879

In consequence of this and after the conclusion of an alliance with Austria, Moltke changed his plan to an offensive against Russia and a defensive against France in the first

THE GERMAN STRATEGIC PLAN 7

instance. He proposed to abandon Alsace and Lorraine if necessary, retiring on the Rhine fortresses and fighting a decisive battle in the Mainz—Frankfurt area behind the Rhine when the French armies would be weakened by the investment of Metz, Strassburg, and Mainz and protection of long lines of communication and crossings over the Rhine. If the French came through Belgium he would strike north at their flank and lines of communication. It will appear later that the German armies in 1914 were weakened by just these factors which were not duly appreciated by the great Moltke's nephew, the leader in 1914.

In Russia the Germans were to attack north of the Vistula bend towards the river Narev and the Austrians at the southern end of the front from eastern Galicia. When Italy came into the Triple Alliance Italian troops were to be used in Alsace. (In 1914: two cavalry divisions and three corps.)

Count von Waldersee, Moltke's successor, adhered to these plans, with the modification that a decisive offensive in Russia would be almost impossible in spring or autumn when the roads become impassable.

PLAN OF 1891

Count von Schlieffen became Chief of the Great General Staff in 1891. His character and military career are of great interest, for it was he who conceived the German plan of campaign put into force in 1914. An interesting insight into Schlieffen's character is given by Kuhl in one of his books. Schlieffen made a habit of setting his subordinate Staff Officers holiday tasks on all festive occasions such as Christmas, for he said that then they could devote their brains to the larger military problems undisturbed by routine work. On one occasion Kuhl brought in his appreciation up to time on Boxing Day and was immediately handed out a second problem to be done on New Year's Day.

Schlieffen was once making a tour of inspection in East

8 GERMAN STRATEGY IN THE GREAT WAR

Prussia when his A.D.C. drew his attention to the beauty of the scenery in a certain valley. Schlieffen looked up and grunted out : " The ground is not suitable for defence, and that river is of no value as a military obstacle," and relapsed into silence again.

He thought of nothing but the German Army and its tasks in war.

Count von Schlieffen retained his predecessor's plan in principle, but changed the front of attack in Russia as he considered the Austrian and the German attacks were too widely separated for decisive results. He proposed combined Austrian and German attacks against the southern and western angle of the Polish salient. It is interesting to compare this decision with the Falkenhayn-Ludendorff controversy on exactly the same subject in 1915, Falkenhayn adhering to Schlieffen's ideas, while Ludendorff was a disciple of the elder Moltke and Waldersee.

SCHLIEFFEN'S FINAL PLAN

In the succeeding years the armies of the Powers increased greatly in size. The areas selected by Moltke in 1879 for the deployment on the west were no longer suitable, and the French might attack in both Lorraine and Belgium instead of in one area only. Considerations of the effect of weather on the operations and supply of vast armies in the east also had greater influence. Schlieffen recognized that a rapid decision against Russia could under no circumstances be reached owing to the lack of vital objectives on the eastern front and the unlimited expanse of territory over which the Russians could retreat if their Field Army was threatened with defeat. An attack in the first instance on Russia with a defence in the west involved a long war and was therefore rejected. It was, therefore, decided to plan a decisive attack in the west as the first operation. The French eastern fortifications still precluded any hope of a rapid advance or victory on the common Franco-German frontier.

THE GERMAN STRATEGIC PLAN

These fortifications had to be outflanked. From the German military aspect, the German Army must go through Belgium. The Germans therefore decided to violate ruthlessly the neutrality of Belgium. Actually the Germans still say that their plan was based on the well-founded assumption that France would not respect Belgian neutrality or else that Belgium would join France.

The first plan combined a frontal attack with the turning movement, but as the necessity for a wider and wider envelopment arose to ensure getting round the French flank, the frontal attack was omitted and the northern enveloping armies pivoting on the fortified area Metz—Thionville were increased to the utmost, leaving a small force for defensive duties only in Lorraine. Schlieffen's plan even included an advance through the Maastricht Peninsula of Holland as well as through Belgium. Schlieffen counted for success on strategic surprise in the large numbers deployed, and on the more rapid effect of attack by envelopment as compared with frontal attack. After the Russo-Japanese war the weakness of the Russians allowed the Germans to use nearly their whole force against France, who was now the principal and most threatening enemy. Only the equivalent of thirteen divisions and two cavalry divisions were to face the Russians. The plans of 1905 allotted no less than the equivalent of seventy-eight divisions and eight cavalry divisions to the armies north of Metz—Thionville. This number includes certain "ersatz" divisions formed on mobilization to be sent forward for the investment of Paris. Only nine divisions and three cavalry divisions in addition to fortress garrisons were left to defend Alsace-Lorraine. (Map II.)

Schlieffen is believed to have intended to include an attack on the Verdun—Belfort front in his war plan in addition to the great outflanking move through Belgium and Holland, as soon as he could organize sufficient new formations. His intention was to stage a perfect "Cannae," complete envelopment on both wings.

10 GERMAN STRATEGY IN THE GREAT WAR

In 1906, during the Moroccan crisis, when Schlieffen pressed for war against France, he was dismissed from the post of Chief of General Staff by the Kaiser.

THE PLAN OF 1914. (MAPS I, II AND VII)

The younger Moltke, a nephew of the Field-Marshal of 1870, succeeded Schlieffen as Chief of General Staff. He was chosen by the Kaiser, presumably for the moral effect of his great name, for he had few of the attributes of a great commander.

In 1914 only the equivalent of twelve and a half divisions and one cavalry division were allotted to the eastern frontier. The Germans counted on the slow rate of mobilization of the Russians. This left the equivalent of eighty-eight divisions and ten cavalry divisions for the western front. Moltke adhered to Schlieffen's plan of a great advance through Belgium, but allotted only the equivalent of sixty-one divisions and seven cavalry divisions to the northern or offensive wing, that is, the five armies wheeling north of Thionville. To the two armies south of Metz he gave the equivalent of twenty-seven divisions and three cavalry divisions.

All formations, active, reserve, landwehr and ersatz, are reduced to the equivalent number of divisions for purposes of comparison. The detailed order of battle is given in Appendix II. In comparing Schlieffen's and Moltke's figures it is well to remember that Schlieffen had nine less active divisions than Moltke, for nine ersatz divisions were organized on an active basis between 1905 and 1914, but Moltke allotted eight of these to his defensive wing.

Moltke, probably quite rightly, omitted an advance through Holland from political considerations. This restricted his lines of advance and may have forced him to reduce the strength of his right wing. The younger Moltke had, therefore, very materially altered Schlieffen's plan of 1905 by weakening the offensive wing by some seventeen

THE GERMAN STRATEGIC PLAN 11

divisions. We shall see that he reduced it still further in his conduct of the operations. It is probable that Moltke was aware of Schlieffen's plan for a " Cannae " by making decisive attacks on both flanks, and he may have considered that in 1914 he had the necessary resources available.

The Plan in Detail

In the east the Germans allotted three active and one reserve corps and one reserve division, i.e. nine divisions and one cavalry division, for the defence of East Prussia, organized as the Eighth Army under Prittwitz. The remaining troops provided the garrisons of the frontier fortresses such as Posen, Thorn, Danzig, Konigsberg, and weak frontier guards along the Polish frontier.

In the west the seven German armies were to concentrate on a front of 250 miles from behind the Dutch frontier in the north down to Neu Breisach in the south. The First Army area was behind the Maastricht Peninsula, Second and Third Armies on the German—Belgium frontier, Fourth Army actually in Luxemburg (a neutral state), Fifth, Sixth and Seventh Armies on the German—French frontier.

The five northern armies were to wheel through Belgium and France, pivoting on the fortified Metz—Thionville area and envelope the left wing of the French armies. Provision was made for seizing Liége by a *coup de main* immediately mobilization was ordered and thus opening the passages across the Meuse. The Belgian Army, in the event of Belgium fighting, was to be dealt with by the First Army and was to be forced away from Antwerp in a westerly direction. The First Army was to be responsible throughout for the protection of the only open flank of the German armies, and the pace of the whole wheel was to be regulated by the rate of advance of the First and Second Armies. As soon as Liége was captured, the right wing armies were to wheel forward to a line Liége—Thionville, after which orders for the general advance would be issued. The most interesting

12 GERMAN STRATEGY IN THE GREAT WAR

part of the plan is the forecast of moves up to the 31st day of mobilization. By the 22nd day, actually 23rd August, the armies were expected to be on a line Ghent—Mons—Sedan—Thionville. Four divisions of the right wing were detailed to seize the Channel ports. Owing to other detachments they were not available in 1914. Kluck with the First Army in 1914 actually got rather ahead of the plan. A very interesting point arises out of this. Kluck's leading corps did not complete detrainment in their concentration area before 12th August. They did not and actually could not advance to Aachen till 13th August. The leading troops of the First Army moved 36 miles on 13th, 14th and 15th August, during which time they crossed the Meuse north of Liége. The advance of the German armies depended on the First Army's pace, so it is hard to see that the general advance could have started any earlier. Yet the protagonists of the Belgians and of the defence of Liége have frequently pointed to the priceless value of the delay imposed by Liége. There appears to have been no delay. (Map II.)

By the 31st day of mobilization (1st September) the German armies were to reach the line Amiens—La Fère—Rethel—Thionville. In 1914 all the armies were up to the time-table, and Kluck was hurrying his army forward two days ahead with the bit in his teeth and, as will appear later, with the reins of the Supreme Command pulled out of their hands.

Now the German plan did not attempt a time-table beyond this point. They were prepared, however, for the French to attempt to hold them on the line Verdun—La Fère—R. Oise—Paris, or Verdun—Rheims—R. Marne—Paris. In either case Paris and the positions to the north and east were to be turned by an advance of the fourteen divisions of the First Army round the west side and to the south of Paris, while the Second Army held the French on the Oise or the Marne down to Paris and attacked them by siege warfare

THE GERMAN STRATEGIC PLAN

methods. In Schlieffen's plan six ersatz corps were to follow the First Army to invest Paris on the west and south, while the First Army reinforced by troops withdrawn from the other armies would push forward in the direction of Auxerre and Troyes and drive the French eastwards against the Swiss frontier.

The dispositions of the German railway troops is interesting. Sixty per cent. of the Railway Construction and Operating Companies were placed to work in rear of the First and Second Armies. After mobilization, sufficient rolling-stock was held in the area Mainz—Frankfurt to entrain three corps at the same time.

The German plan appears on first examination to be simple, bold and far-reaching with good prospect of success. It was, moreover, in accordance with the German teaching of strategy, envelopment at all costs.

However, this plan had the effect of bringing Belgium and Great Britain into the scale against them owing to the violation of Belgian neutrality. Italy remained neutral. In fact, it put Germany in the wrong in the eyes of the world.

Observations Regarding the Plan

It would be of great interest to discover why Moltke strengthened his defensive wing at the expense of his main operation. He thereby went far to ruin the plan prepared by his able predecessor Schlieffen, described by Ludendorff as "one of the greatest soldiers who ever lived."

Moltke's plan, of course, maintained the neutrality of Holland which Schlieffen had apparently intended to violate. But the principal difference between the two conceptions lay in Moltke omitting from the right wing the ersatz formations intended to follow in rear of the armies and only to reach the front at Paris. Moltke could, probably, have carried these moves out without requiring any greater front to deploy on, and could therefore have maintained the

14   GERMAN STRATEGY IN THE GREAT WAR

strength of the right wing without marching across the Maastricht Peninsula.

Moltke presumably intended to avoid all risk of invasion of Alsace-Lorraine, but in doing so he violated some of the principles of war—concentration at the decisive point—in that he had not the strength in his offensive wing to envelope the French armies without allowing gaps to arise in his own armies – and economy of force – in that his detachments south of Metz failed to hold the French forces there. It may be considered, judging by after events, that this violation of principles lost the war.

Schlieffen clearly recognized the vital part of his plan, and even as he lay dying, he murmured to his son-in-law, General von Hahnke—"It must come to a fight. Only make the right wing strong!"

The question of the capacity of German Supreme Command to control seven armies on a 300-mile front in the west, and another army with various detachments in the east, is another problem for consideration. It would appear far sounder to have organized the Western Front into two or three army groups and the Eastern Front under one group.

The plan of mobilization and deployment for a great army, once formed, cannot be altered at short notice. When once the Great Powers in 1914 had ordered mobilization, war was inevitable. This is proved by Moltke's argument with the Kaiser on 31st July, 1914. As the result of some misunderstanding the German Ambassador in London wired that England would undertake to keep France out of the war, if Germany would engage not to undertake any hostilities against France. On this the Kaiser said to Moltke: "Now we need only to wage war against Russia. Then we will simply deploy the whole army in the east."

Moltke replied: "Your Majesty, that is impossible, it means a whole laborious year's work, and once settled, cannot be changed. If your Majesty insists on leading the

THE GERMAN STRATEGIC PLAN 15

whole army to the east, it will not be an army ready for battle, but a useless agglomeration of dislocated armed men without supplies."

The Kaiser replied : " Your uncle would have given me a different answer." And Moltke records that this hurt him greatly !

However, this conversation shows the Kaiser's ignorance of the larger operations of war, and also that Moltke was prepared to stand up to the " Supreme War Lord."

CHAPTER III

THE FRONTIER BATTLES ON THE WESTERN FRONT

THE GERMAN ADVANCE IN THE WEST (Map III)

The operations on the western front in August and the first half of September, 1914, are clearly divided into two zones by the fortresses of Metz and Verdun. Between these two fortresses along the Meuse Heights the battle front did not fluctuate 10 miles either way in the whole of this period.

To the west there occurred the great drama of the German advance through northern France, culminating in the battle of the Marne and the retreat to the Aisne. Here neither side fought out the battles to the end, each army in turn escaping by retreat from the dangerous position in which the errors of their high command had placed them.

To the east of Metz there occurred three separate operations, less thrilling and apparently less decisive than the rapidly changing events on the west, but which in fact led to the downfall of the German war plan and the saving of France. First the advance by the French to the river Nied in Lorraine, then the counter-attack by the Germans, their advance to the Trouée de Charmes and defeat there, and finally their fruitless and costly attacks on the Grand Couronné de Nancy; these were the events which were the main cause of the German defeat on the Marne.

To return for a moment to Schlieffen's plan. His conception was to seize the initiative from the outset of the campaign by an advance in overwhelming strength on the

THE FRONTIER BATTLES 17

western wing. By ensuring the success of this move, he maintained that he would force the French to move troops to the area where the menace was greatest—that is, to Paris—and that he could therefore disregard the initial French concentration. He intended to carry out one continuous operation with the object of a decisive battle in the Paris area, and his dispositions were made to ensure success there.

Now Moltke's conception of the German plan differed considerably. He regarded the enveloping move through Belgium merely as a means of drawing the French armies away from the support of their fortified areas, and he was prepared to fight the decisive battle wherever fate or the French led him. It might be about Paris, or it might be in Lorraine, and he apparently rather inclined to the latter area, influenced by a knowledge of the French concentration and war plan. He believed the French were going to attack in Lorraine south of Metz with all their forces.

Moltke himself, therefore, seems to have started the war with Schlieffen's plan but without Schlieffen's singleness of purpose, and we shall see how his mind swayed like a feather in the wind from one plan to the other.

On mobilization Moltke took counsel with his fears, and sent the ersatz divisions, intended to join Kluck for the investment of Paris, to the Lorraine front.

THE OPERATIONS OF THE SIXTH AND SEVENTH GERMAN ARMIES

On 9th August the Sixth and Seventh Armies were placed under the orders of Crown Prince Rupprecht, the Sixth Army Commander. He had two rôles—first, to protect the left flank of the German offensive wing by preventing a French penetration between Metz and Strassburg; secondly, to hold on his front all the French troops assembling there. Now he could carry out the first rôle by acting with small forces on the defensive on the prepared river Nied position between Metz and Saarburg. The second rôle he could only execute by attacking the French. If he attacked successfully, a very short advance would bring his armies face to face with the great line of French fortresses and his efforts might be wasted, for it was to be expected that the fortresses would hold his seventeen first line divisions and at the same time release as many French troops as Joffre cared to move. It is easy to be wise after the event, but Crown Prince Rupprecht appears to have had small prospects of success in his two tasks, while the first task could have been carried out with less troops.

The first event was the advance of a French corps into Alsace on 7th August, to Mulhausen and Cernay, whence they were driven back on the 9th August by two German corps (XIV and XV of Seventh Army). Rupprecht then intended the Sixth and Seventh German Armies to take the offensive towards the Moselle and the Meurthe to fulfil his dual rôle. However, by 14th August, when his armies were assembled in readiness, it was realized at Supreme Command that the French were assembling in great strength between the Vosges and Metz (actually twenty-four divisions, First and Second French Armies). It appeared that Moltke's ideas were going to prove correct and that the mass of the French armies were there and he envisaged a decisive battle in Lorraine. A German attack here against superior numbers before the northern wing could make its weight felt would, however, be premature, so Rupprecht was told to withdraw towards the Saar so as to lead the French away from their fortresses.

Moltke then prepared the stage for his great battle in Lorraine. The French were to be held upon the Nied position, the Seventh Army was to attack them from the east (Strassburg), the Sixth to attack across the Nied, the Fifth Army from Metz and east of it, while the Fourth Army marched south and completed the envelopment. After a decisive victory here, Moltke intended to transfer the bulk of the Sixth and Seventh Armies to the right wing for the

THE FRONTIER BATTLES

second and final battle in northern France, and there was for this purpose the mass of rolling-stock already collected on the railways behind the Lorraine front.

By the 17th August, however, it became clear to Supreme Command that the mass of the French armies were not being drawn into Lorraine and that there were many French divisions collecting west of the Meuse about Mézières and north of it (twenty divisions, Fourth and Fifth French Armies). Moltke hastily reverted to Schlieffen's plan and ordered the Fourth and Fifth German Armies to resume their place in the northern wing whose advance was to commence from the line west of Liége—Thionville on 18th August.

THE BATTLE IN LORRAINE, 20TH–23RD AUGUST

On 19th August the French reached the Nied position between Saarburg and Metz and the following morning attempted to assault it practically without artillery support, for their unopposed advance had led them to expect little opposition. However, the German heavy batteries and the machine-guns of the Landwehr garrison checked them with deadly effect.

Rupprecht meanwhile, left to his own devices by Moltke's change of plan, reverted to his ideas of attack. Foerster in his book, *Graf Schlieffen und der Weltkrieg*, says that—" Rupprecht raised objections to the continuance of the retirement when everybody else was going forward. He also wanted to attack, and the Supreme Command let him." Those last few words give the clue to all Moltke's dealings with his Army Commanders.

So on the 20th August the Sixth and Seventh Armies advanced, directed on the headwaters of the river Meurthe. They met the French about midday in the middle of their attack on the Nied position. The French Second Army received the heaviest blow about Morhange and to the north-west and retired to a position 12 miles in rear. During the night it retired further and exposing the left and rear of the First French Army caused its withdrawal.

Meanwhile events in the north had shown Joffre that his initial concentration was utterly unsuitable to meet the German advance, and, on the 19th August, he ordered two corps from the French Second Army to move north to the Mézières area and on the 20th he ordered both First and Second Armies to withdraw to the fortified line Epinal—Nancy. These moves were ordered irrespective of the results of the Battle of Lorraine and were due to the seizure of the initiative by the Germans in the north. (Map I.)

Here was a golden opportunity for Moltke to carry out to the letter Schlieffen's plan. There was now no fear of invasion of Lorraine and he could have used his rolling-stock waiting on the railways to move troops north to ensure the success of his enveloping movement, but his mind was still held by the mirage of a victory in Lorraine and he allowed Rupprecht to pursue the French in the south. By 23rd August the French armies were back across the frontier.

THE WHEEL THROUGH BELGIUM. (MAP III.)

To turn to the events on the northern wing. All went according to plan in the north, the last of the Liége forts fell on 17th August and during the siege the German armies had got to their starting line, Liége—Thionville, ready for the general advance on 18th August. Apparently Joffre did not even now realize the extent of the German movement. He ordered his Third and Fourth Armies to attack from about Sedan and Montmedy into Belgian Luxemburg against the flank of the German forces in Belgium. The French Fifth and British Armies were to co-operate on the Sambre. Portions of the German Third, Fourth and Fifth Armies, amounting to some twenty-four divisions, met the seventeen divisions of the French Third and Fourth Armies and drove them out of the Ardennes and back to the Meuse by the 24th August. Meantime the First, Second and Third German

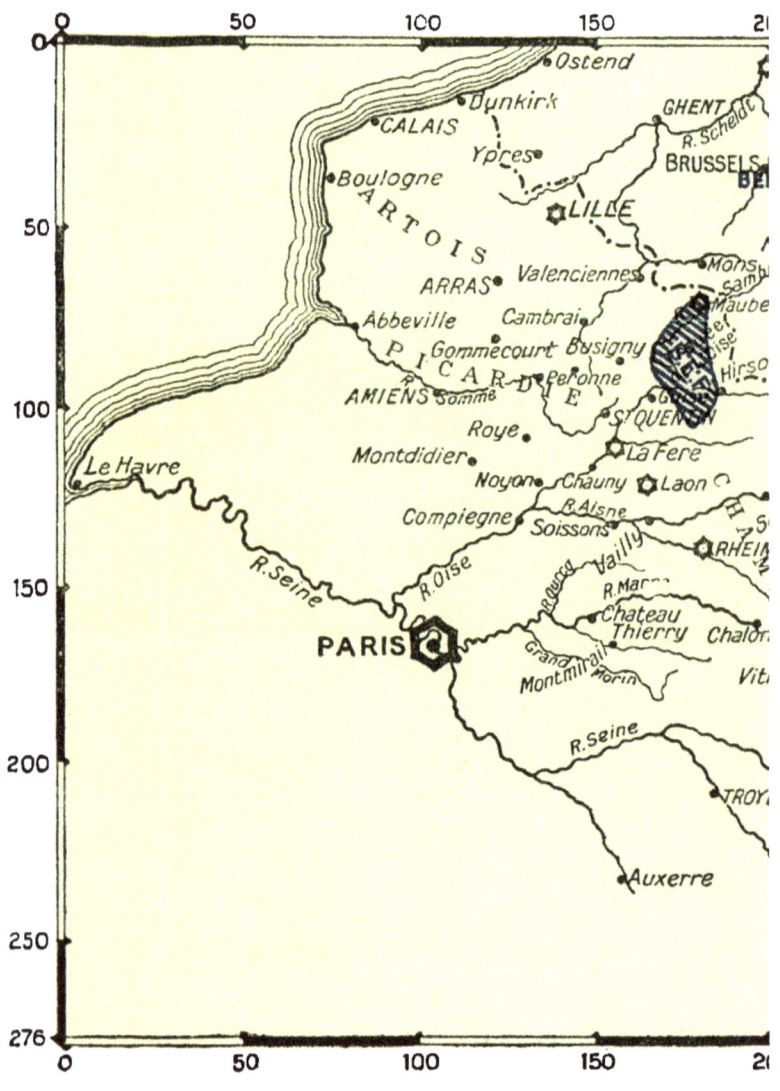

CONCENTRATION AREAS ON TH
GERMAN ARMIES IN RED: EN

MAP I

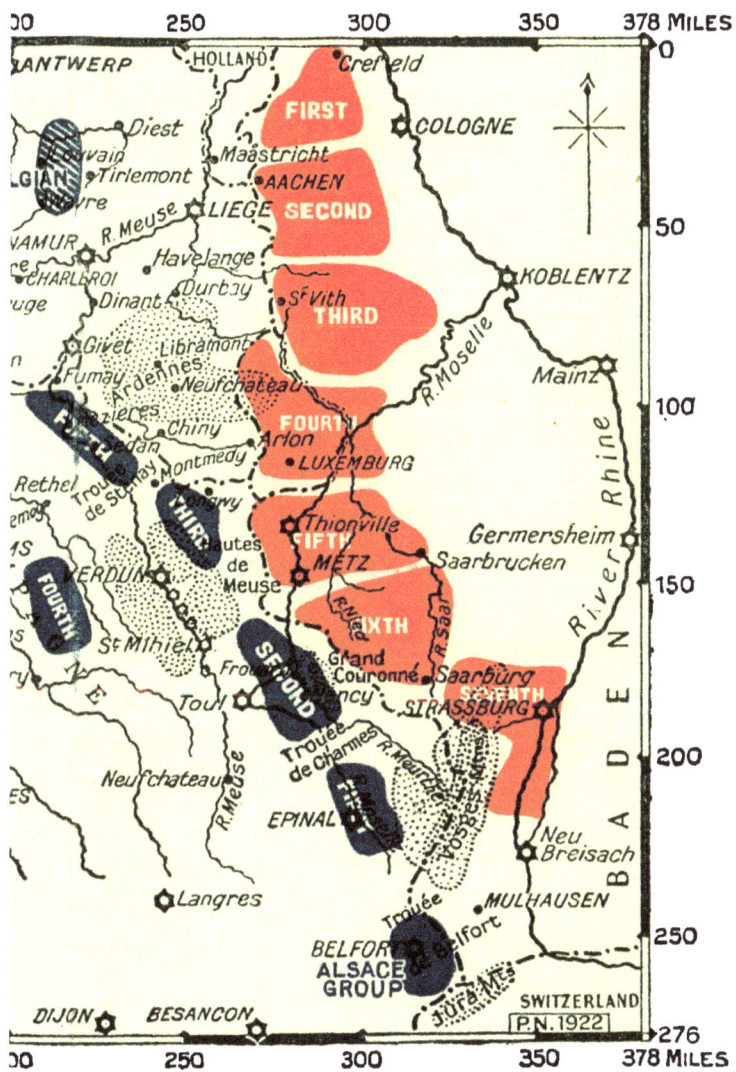

THE WESTERN FRONT, 1914
ENTENTE ARMIES IN BLUE

Armies (twenty-six divisions at this time) drove forward on to the isolated British and Fifth French Armies (seventeen divisions). This German attack lost a great opportunity of completely cutting off the *Entente* forces (actually they thought there were no British troops there). Supreme Command ordered a co-ordinated attack by Bülow's Second Army against the Namur—Charleroi line and Hausen's Third Army against the Namur—Givet front, but left the Army Commanders to arrange the date, which was fixed for 23rd August. However, Bülow thought there was little to oppose his advance and crossed the Sambre on 22nd, thereby showing his strength to the French, who thereupon immediately retreated from their perilous position and were able to regain touch with their Fourth Army.

The fatal detachments from the German right wing armies had continued during this phase. The Guard Reserve Corps and XI Corps had been detached from Second and Third Armies to mask and besiege Namur and when they were freed by its fall on 23rd August they were at once dispatched to Russia, where they arrived after the crisis of invasion had passed. The III Reserve and IX Reserve Corps had been detached from the First Army to mask Antwerp and were kept there till the fortress fell on 10th October.

The 24th Reserve Division was detached from the Third Army to capture Givet and only reached the front during the battle of the Marne.

It is desirable to try and appreciate the effect on Supreme Command of the three battles on the French frontier between 20th and 23rd August, that is, the Battles of Lorraine, the Ardennes, and Charleroi—Mons. By the 25th August Moltke considered " that the great decisive battle in the west had been fought and decided in Germany's favour, and that the moment had arrived when forces might be sent to the eastern front." These are the words of Maj.-Gen. von Tappen, Moltke's Director of Military Operations. This opinion was so decided that six corps were ordered to Russia, one from each army except the First. Subsequent events led to only two corps going and these, as we know, came from the striking wing.

Moltke, at his headquarters in Koblentz, 200 miles from the scene of battle, was entirely dependent on the reports of his Army Commanders to gauge the extent of the victories.

Actually in every case the battle had been broken off and the French and British armies had withdrawn, with severe losses it is true, but with their organization and fighting power intact.

The Attack on the Trouée de Charmes, 25th–27th August

Moltke's next plan was to break through the French eastern fortifications at the Trouée de Charmes between Epinal and Toul in the hope of achieving a double envelopment of the French armies between Nancy and Paris. To this end the Sixth and Seventh Armies pressed forward on 24th and 25th August to try and cross the Moselle.

Their attack was met by Dubail's First French Army and De Castelnau's Second French Army with a very clever manœuvre and use of ground.

De Castelnau on the north turned the right flank of his army back from the Grand Couronné de Nancy in a southerly direction to the Moselle, while Dubail in the south turned the left flank of his army back from the bastions of the Vosges in a westerly direction astride the Meurthe to the Forest of Charmes on the Moselle.

The Trouée de Charmes, a level gap some 12 miles wide, was where they met, one army facing east and the other north and each with their centre and one flank on a very strong position. Whichever army the Germans attacked, the other could counter-attack the Germans in flank.

The Germans attacked in a southerly direction on 26th August. The Seventh Army on the Vosges and the Sixth Army on the Charmes Gap presenting their flank to Nancy,

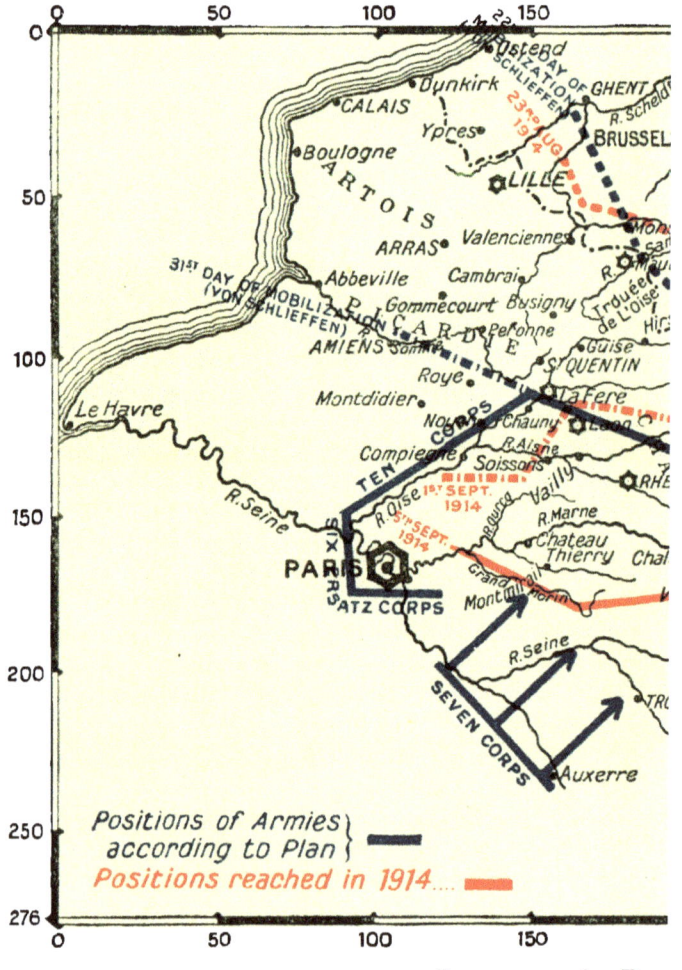

MAP II

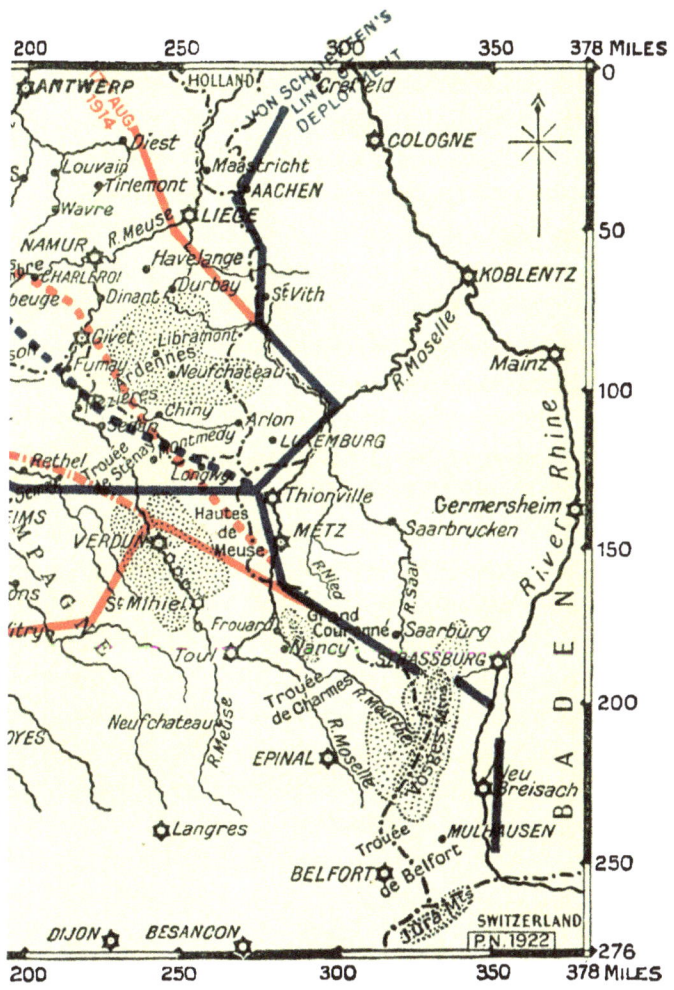

THE FRONTIER BATTLES

The French held up the Seventh German Army east of the Meurthe and attacked the Sixth German Army frontally from the south and in flank from the west from Nancy. The counter-offensive was successful and the German attack was broken by the 27th. It is noteworthy that the decisive flank attack was delivered by the XX French Corps under Foch from Nancy, and that Dubail and De Castelnau had made an artificial salient for the Germans to run their heads into.

This battle of the Trouée de Charmes had a great effect on Moltke's decisions regarding the sending of troops to Russia. Moltke wrote in a report on these operations that the losses had been so heavy that he could not take units from the Seventh Army which he had intended to do, and instead took them from the right wing. He ends by saying, " I admit that this was a mistake and one that was fully paid for on the Marne."

It is therefore safe to say that the defence of the Charmes Gap directly caused the absence of two German Corps from the Marne. While, on the other hand, the Germans did not prevent Joffre taking troops from this front to the Marne. The Crown Prince Rupprecht and the German left wing had failed in one of their tasks.

CHAPTER IV

THE CHANGE IN THE GERMAN PLAN OF CAMPAIGN

THE BATTLE OF GUISE—ST. QUENTIN, 29TH–30TH AUGUST.
(MAPS III AND IV.)

The failure of German Supreme Command to co-ordinate the action of its right wing armies cropped up again and again during the advance. Their directions for the march of the armies were in very vague and general terms, whereas such an operation involving a vast wheel through more than ninety degrees should require careful instructions regarding the frontage or boundaries of each army. The results of this failure appeared on 26th August when the Third Army began to edge away from the Second Army, moving in a southerly direction instead of south-west. This was accentuated on 28th August when the Fourth Army, becoming involved in heavy fighting south of Sedan, demanded assistance by wireless and the Third Army wheeled south-eastwards accordingly, increasing the gap between it and Bülow's army.

To make matters worse, the only attempt at co-ordination, the control of Kluck's First Army by Bülow since August 18th, was terminated on 27th August by order of Supreme Command in response to a wireless appeal by Kluck. The next day Kluck directed his army away to the west apparently with the avowed object of surrounding the British Army and Bülow complained, " My army was thus threatened with isolation." That this was no idle fear appeared during the battle of Guise—St. Quentin on 29th August, when the Fifth French Army halted and counter-attacked

THE CHANGE IN THE GERMAN PLAN 25

Bülow. On that day there appears to have been a gap of 20 miles between Bülow and Hausen and 15 miles between Bülow and Kluck.

Bülow at once wirelessed to both Hausen and Kluck to march to his assistance. This seems to have been an accepted method of co-ordinating the German armies in battle, Supreme Command remaining silent.

Meantime, on 28th August, Supreme Command sent out a general order for the further conduct of the campaign. At the time of issue Kluck was on the Somme, Maricourt—Peronne—Nesle. In this order Moltke adhered to the original plan of campaign to encircle Paris on the west. (Map IV.)

The First Army was directed west of Paris to the Seine with its left on the Oise, and was given two rôles—to co-operate in the fighting of the Second Army and to protect the flank of the armies.

Second Army was directed on Paris via La Fère—Laon.

Third Army was directed on Chateau Thierry, Fourth Army on Epernay, Fifth Army on Chalons—Vitry le Francois with left flank echelonned back to protect the flank of the armies until the Sixth Army could take over this duty. Verdun was to be invested.

Sixth and Seventh Armies were directed on to the line Neufchateau—Epinal—Belfort in the event of the French withdrawing. The possibility of a change of direction to the south in case of serious opposition on the Aisne or the Marne was indicated and finally a rapid advance was urged to give the French no time to reorganize and offer serious resistance. The last sentence indicates Supreme Command's opinion of the condition of the French Army.

Now this order anticipated the armies getting on to the line Swiss frontier—Belfort—Epinal—Neufchateau—Vitry le Francois—thence the line of the Marne to Paris with the First Army enveloping Paris on the west, a frontage of 300 miles for the seven armies. Actually when the armies reached and crossed the Marne the frontage from the Swiss frontier Grand Couronné—Verdun—Vitry le Francois to Paris and west of Paris would have been 360 miles, an additional 60 miles if this order had been carried out.

Meantime, however, an additional corps had been detached from the rapidly diminishing right wing for the investment of Maubeuge.

KLUCK'S SOUTH-EAST WHEEL. (MAP III.)

On 30th August, Kluck's much discussed inward wheel commenced in response primarily to Bülow's appeal for help. In accordance with one of his rôles ordered by Supreme Command he went to co-operate in the fighting of the Second Army. On 31st he wheeled still further in order to try and attack the Fifth French Army in flank and rear, again in response to Bülow's request. On 30th August he informed Supreme Command by wireless of his intended move towards Compiègne.

Bülow insists in his book that this move was only intended as a temporary tactical measure and was by no means an attempt to abandon the plans laid down in the last Supreme Command order.

However, during the night of 30th August Supreme Command issued instructions approving Kluck's inward wheel and giving fresh objectives to the Second and Third Armies in a south-east and southerly direction. Second Army with its left on Rheims, Third Army towards the line Rethel—Semoy. This order ignores the assembly of the French Sixth Army which had been trying to concentrate in the Amiens area and was now moving south to Paris, although the assembly and identification had been duly reported.

The German war plan had now been definitely abandoned. The reason for this is a matter of great interest and considerable uncertainty. It is hardly conceivable that even Moltke could feebly accept a *fait accompli* by one of his Army Commanders.

The fact was that the stubborn defence of Verdun and the

THE CHANGE IN THE GERMAN PLAN   27

passages of the Meuse north of it had been drawing the Fifth Army ever further east and the Fourth Army had had to conform, in fact these two armies had been unable to keep their place in the wheel. Then, as we have seen, the Third Army had diverted its march to the south-east to help the Fourth south of Sedan. A reference to Map No. III will show that by 29th August the First and Second German Armies were getting isolated. The fact was, the Germans had not enough troops in their right flank armies to carry out their plan. The loss of eleven divisions, for that was the total detachments (not counting the *ersatz* divisions which had never joined this wing), had ruined their plan. On 30th August the German Armies were on a front of some 280 miles, with gaps already of approximately 20 miles between First and Second Armies, 20 miles between Second and Third, and nearly 20 miles between Third and Fourth. Adherence to the original plan meant an increase of front to 300 miles as a minimum and possibly to 360 miles.

The surprising thing is that this only became evident to Supreme Command between the evening of the 28th August when orders were issued in accordance with the war plan, and the evening of the 30th August when the inward wheel was approved of. It appears probable that the battle of Guise—St. Quentin on 29th and 30th August brought home to Supreme Command the fact that their three right wing armies were beyond supporting distance from each other.

It appears that Kluck and presumably also Moltke genuinely thought that the British Army was out of the war for the time being and could be ignored. In spite of this they could not claim to be enveloping the left flank of the main French armies according to plan, for the Sixth French Army began to make its appearance further west about Amiens from 29th August onwards. It is possible that the composition of this army, principally reserve divisions, influenced Moltke. He may have thought it incapable of offensive action.

28 GERMAN STRATEGY IN THE GREAT WAR

The fact is, the Germans could not help themselves and were guilty of bad strategy in attempting a plan beyond their means. The means being insufficient owing to Moltke's obsession regarding Lorraine. After Supreme Command order of 28th August, Moltke appears to have paid little heed to his right wing until the Battle of the Marne forced it upon his notice. To quote a biting criticism of Moltke :—
" He trusted to the weary feet of his right wing armies to capture Paris rather than to the brains of Supreme Command."

Moltke's first error was in allotting an ultimate total of twenty-seven divisions to Lorraine on mobilization instead of Schlieffen's nine. His second error was in allowing Rupprecht to attack the Trouée de Charmes on 26th August instead of transferring one of his armies to the western wing. His third error was in sending two corps from the western wing to Russia, and his fourth error was his attempt from 4th to 8th September to break through the fortified area of the French right wing.

GERMAN OFFENSIVE AGAINST FRENCH RIGHT WING, 4TH TO 8TH SEPTEMBER

The news of the reverse at the Trouée de Charmes caused consternation at Supreme Command. In view of the great strategical effect of a break-through on the Moselle, after long discussion it was decided to continue the offensive there. So Moltke planned a great *coup* around Verdun. The advance of the Fifth Army west of Verdun to the upper Marne would, he believed, turn the Verdun—Nancy defences and cause the enemy to withdraw. So he combined this with a fresh advance by the Sixth Army on the Trouée de Charmes, and to safeguard this advance he ordered the assault of the Grand Couronné. On 30th August seventy heavy batteries were ordered forward from Metz, Strassburg and the Nied to assist.

The Fifth Army, however, as we have seen, was being drawn eastwards against Verdun instead of getting in

THE CHANGE IN THE GERMAN PLAN 29

rear of the Verdun—Nancy position. Moltke tried to remedy this by urging the Third and Fourth Armies to renewed efforts directed in a south-easterly direction. Paris and the French left flank was forgotten, Verdun—Nancy were the aim. On 3rd September, First and Second Armies also were ordered to force the enemy in a south-easterly direction away from Paris with the First Army *in echelon behind* the Second. At the time of issue of the order the First Army was across the Marne nearly a day's march *ahead* of the Second Army with only one corps in rear for flank protection.

It was not till 4th September that Moltke awoke to the threat to his right flank from the French Army assembling at Paris, although the movement had been identified a week before. On this day he definitely turned to his own plan of two decisive battles—first one on the east flank, and then one on the west to deal with the enemy about Paris.

It appears from the opening paragraph of his order of 4th September, that Moltke had a fairly clear idea of the general situation. This read as follows :—

" 4th September.—7.45 p.m. (To all the Armies.)

" The enemy has evaded the enveloping attack of the First and Second Armies, and a part of his force has joined up with those about Paris. From reports and other information, it appears that the enemy is moving troops westwards from the front Toul—Belfort, and is also taking them from the front of the Third, Fourth and Fifth Armies. The attempt to force the whole French Army back in a south-easterly direction towards the Swiss frontier is thus rendered impracticable and the new situation to be appreciated shows that the enemy is bringing up new formations and concentrating superior forces in the neighbourhood of Paris, to protect the capital and to threaten the right flank of the German Army."

To gain time for the first battle the First and Second Armies were ordered to turn and face the east front of Paris,

First Army between Oise and Marne, Second Army between Marne and Seine.

This portion of the order bore no relation to the existing position of the troops or to any possibility of carrying it out. Gen. Baumgarten-Crusuis made a comment on it worth quoting :—" Ordered too late, impossible to carry out; the directions of O.H.L. (Supreme Command) which was established too far to the rear, break down more and more and fate takes its course."

Moreover, Lt.-Col. Hentsch, who took the order to the First German Army, indicated that there was no urgent hurry to take up the new dispositions. Hentsch was the O.H.L. liaison officer. In spite of the opening paragraph of this order, O.H.L. did not appreciate the danger.

The order goes on to indicate the plan for the decisive attack on the French right wing by the remaining five German armies, three armies on the line Verdun—Chalons and two armies on the line Nancy—Epinal with the object of destroying the French in the area Chalons—Nancy—Verdun.

On the 4th, 5th and 8th September Rupprecht hurled his divisions trained only in open warfare against the prepared positions of the Grand Couronné de Nancy as a preparatory measure to advancing on the Charmes Gap. The attacks were in vain, although at one time de Castelnau was nearly forced to retreat.

On the evening of the 8th, Supreme Command ordered the attacks to cease, defensive positions to be prepared in rear, and all available units to be prepared to move to the right wing of the armies. The offensive of the German Third, Fourth and Fifth Armies had been equally unsuccessful. This was the end of Moltke's first battle.

His second battle had been started for him by his enemies and he appears to have taken no part in directing the Battle of the Marne nor to have realized its importance, for there is no trace of any orders to the right wing armies from 4th September until they were ordered to retreat on 9th September.

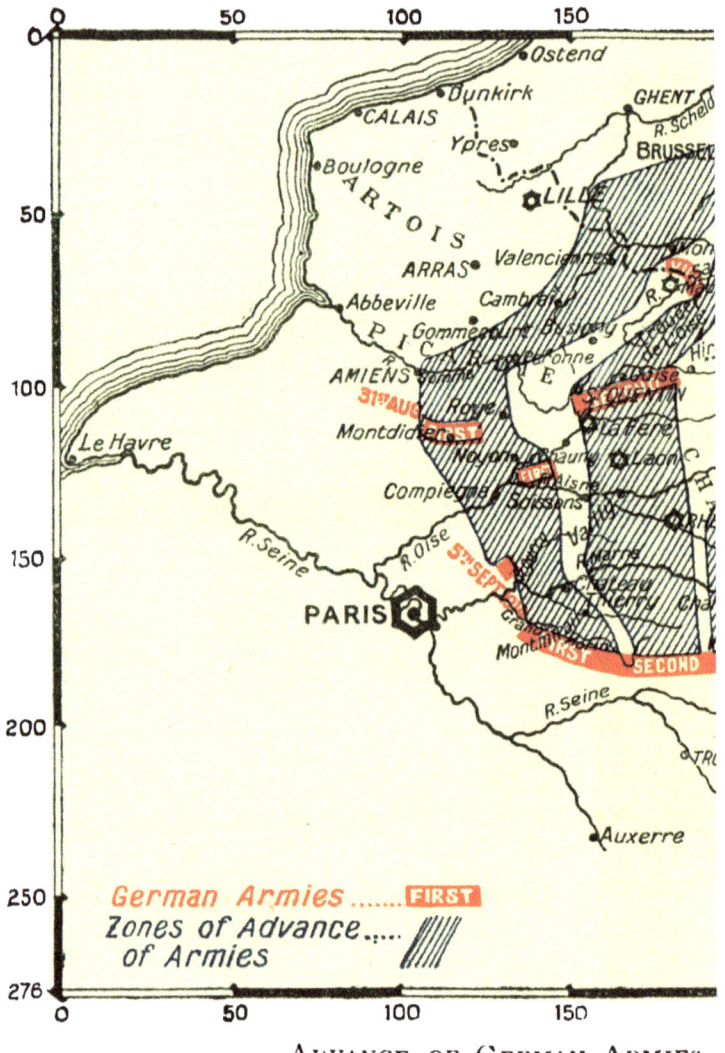

ADVANCE OF GERMAN ARMIES

MAP III

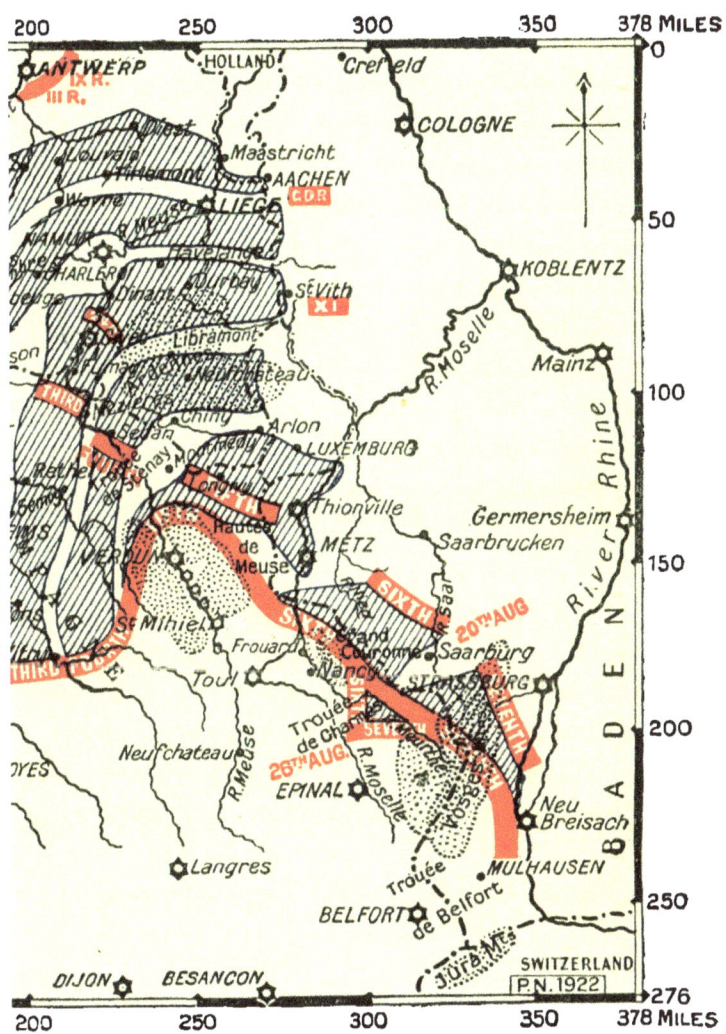

UP TO 5TH SEPTEMBER, 1914

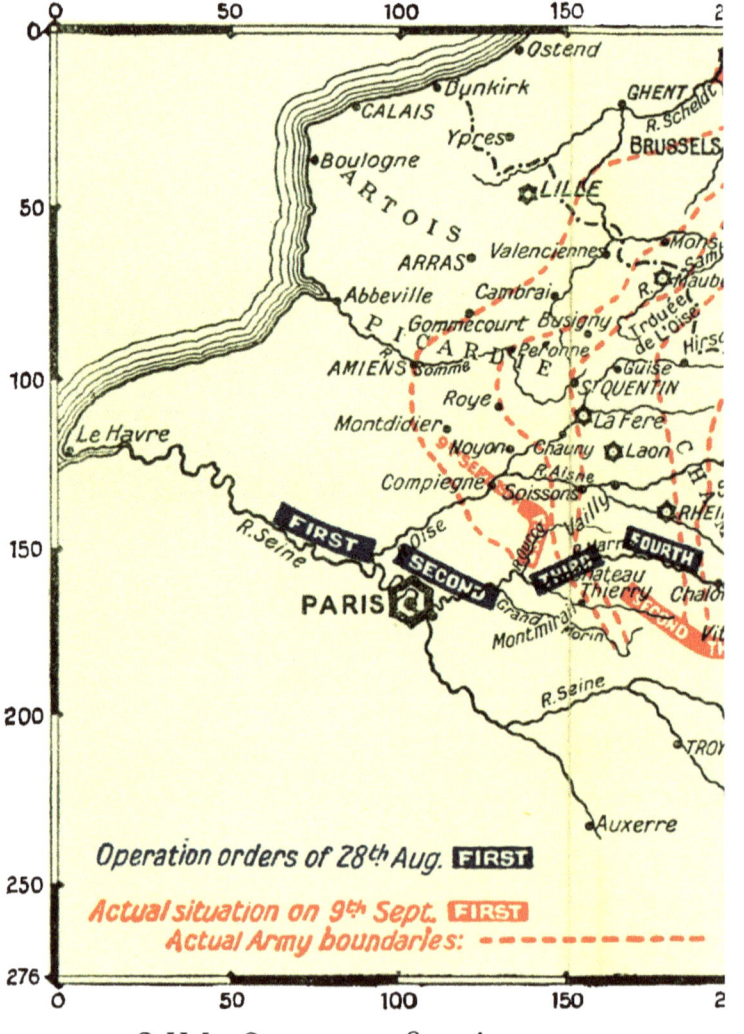

O.H.L. Order of 28th August, 1914, for

MAP IV

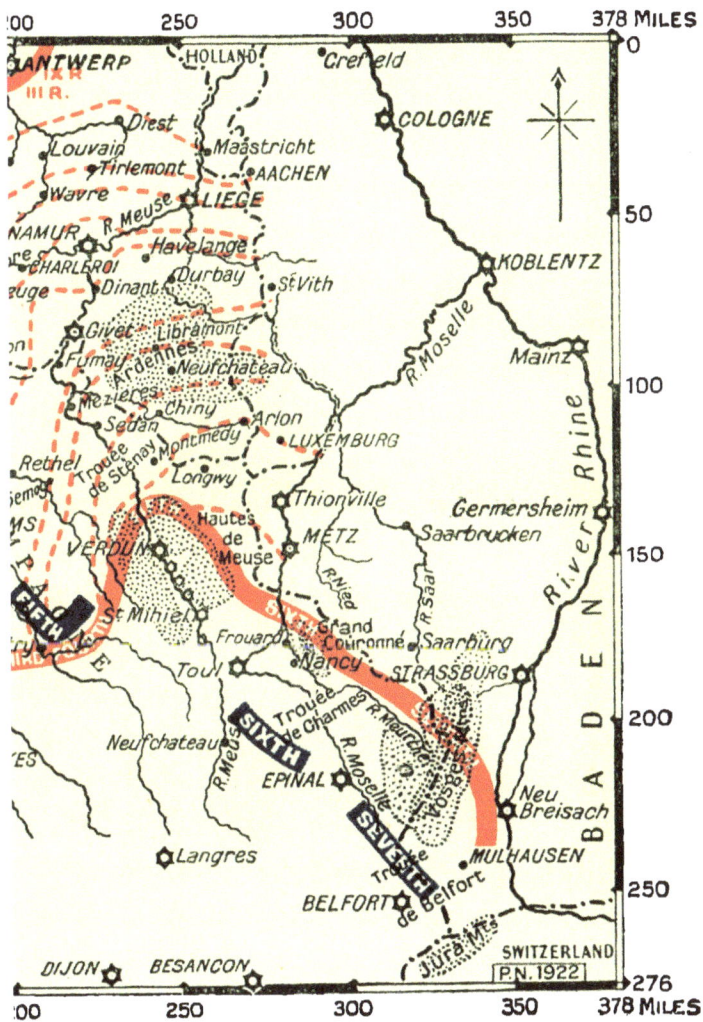

FURTHER CONDUCT OF THE CAMPAIGN

CHAPTER V

BATTLE OF THE MARNE AND EVENTS IN THE WEST TO THE END OF 1914

THE BATTLE OF THE MARNE. (MAP V.)

In point of fact the French from 29th August onwards had been moving very large forces to their left wing undeterred by the German efforts on the eastern wing, and by the 5th September had formed a fresh army, the Sixth, on their left, which with the British and the Fifth Army already there, and the Ninth Army formed from a portion of the Fourth already in line, formed a mass of some twenty-eight divisions to attack the right wing of the Germans who now had only some twenty divisions to face this on their First, Second and right flank of their Third Army. Moreover, the Germans had a gap of 13 miles between their right flank guard and their main forces on 5th September which increased to 28 miles on 6th September when Von Kluck moved his army to the Ourcq to face the French enveloping attack.

On the other wing, the Germans were attacking frontally with some thirty-eight divisions against thirty-three French divisions, most of whom were protected by permanent fortifications or prepared positions.

This situation throws an illuminating light on the conduct of the German higher command in the opening campaign. For years their strategical doctrine had been attack by envelopment. Their whole war plan had aimed at avoiding any attack on the French eastern fortresses and their whole training had been in attack in open warfare. Now when the crisis had been reached, the bulk of the

German armies were delivering frontal attacks on these very frontier fortresses against the French whose strong positions made up for their numerical weakness, while the French were delivering an enveloping attack against far weaker German forces in the open.

The result of the battles of the two wings gave the victory to the *Entente*, saved Paris and saved the *Entente* armies.

The Hentsch Episode and the Retreat

On the 8th September Supreme Command sent one of their Staff Officers, Lt.-Col. Hentsch of the Intelligence Section, to find out the situation and co-ordinate the action of their right wing. He motored to the headquarters of the Fifth, Fourth, Third, Second and First Armies in turn with the following verbal instructions :—" In case rearward movements had already been initiated on the right wing, he was instructed so to direct them that the gap between the First and Second Armies would be again closed, the First Army going, if possible, in the direction of Soissons."

Lt.-Col. Hentsch was, therefore, authorized in the specified circumstances to give binding instructions in the name of the Supreme Command.

Hentsch spent the night of 8th–9th September at Second Army Headquarters. Late on the 8th September, the French Fifth Army succeeded in breaking the front of Bülow's right flank division which was forced back in the Battle of Montmirail. As a result of this and of the situation early on 9th when French and British troops were about to penetrate the 30-mile gap between him and Kluck, Bülow thought he must retreat. This gap was covered only by four German cavalry divisions and a small force of infantry, seven or eight battalions. Hentsch agreed to the decision and went on to the First Army to order their retreat also in the name of Supreme Command. Before Hentsch arrived at First Army Headquarters, a wireless message had already been received from Bülow that the Second Army

BATTLE OF THE MARNE 33

was beginning to retreat behind the Marne. It appears also that Kluck had begun to move back his left wing to face the British penetration before Hentsch arrived at First Army Headquarters.

Thus began the German retreat from the Marne.

Col. Hentsch is dead. He died in Rumania in 1917. Since the war several German writers have tried to throw all the blame for the retreat from the Marne on to Hentsch's shoulders, obviously in order to whitewash the Great General Staff. It is clear that the decision to retreat was made by Bülow, also that the left wing of the First Army had begun to retreat uninfluenced by Hentsch, who carried out his mission of co-ordination correctly.

Hentsch foresaw this, as is proved by the following evidence of two Staff Officers who accompanied Hentsch on his mission to the armies: "He complained during the motor journey to the Front that he had been given no written instructions whatever, and said that in case of defeat he would certainly be made the scapegoat. He expressed himself very strongly that on such an occasion, when the decision might have far-reaching consequences, Gen. von Moltke, Gen. von Stein, Col. Tappen, or at least an officer of the operations section, should have been sent to the armies; on the contrary, he had been selected by design. He had failed to get instructions in writing."

It seems a strange way of controlling the destiny of a vast army for the power of great decisions to be put into the hands of a comparatively junior Staff Officer; think of the weight of responsibility on his shoulders. The fact was, that in order that the Great General Staff might remain infallible, a junior officer was, if necessary, to be sacrificed.

MOLTKE AS A COMMANDER

Helmuth Johannes von Moltke was born in 1848. He was the nephew of the great Field-Marshal who led the Prussians to victory in 1866 and the Germans to victory in 1870. The nephew took part in the war of 1870–71 as an infantry subaltern. Subsequently he was A.D.C. to his uncle and on the death of the Field-Marshal in 1891 he became personal A.D.C. to the Kaiser.

On 1st January, 1904, the Kaiser appointed the younger Moltke to be one of the two Deputy Chiefs of the General Staff, deputy to Schlieffen. It soon became clear that he would be Schlieffen's successor. Although Stein, who was Moltke's deputy in 1914, records that " Moltke had never expected to be C.G.S., had never prepared for it."

At all events, in 1905, the Kaiser told Moltke :—" Graf Schlieffen, when I asked him, said that he had observed you for a year and could suggest no better successor than you."

Apparently Gen. von der Goltz, who died at Baghdad, and Gen. von Beseler, the captor of Antwerp, were also in the running. But the former, the Kaiser disliked—for he had brains—and the latter " he did not know "—for he was an Engineer officer and the Kaiser " knew " only Guard and Cavalry officers.

Now that Moltke was practically nominated as future Chief of General Staff, he took the Kaiser to task on the subject of the training of the army for future war. He thought the army was being trained in view of a single great battle which would end the war and ascribed this doctrine to the fact that the Kaiser, who took part in war games and manœuvres as commander of one side, always had to be victorious. As a fact, Graf Schlieffen had given instructions that :—" When the Kaiser plays, he must win, he cannot as Kaiser be beaten by one of his generals."

Moltke's view of a future war, which he put plainly before the Kaiser in 1905, was :—" a long, wearisome struggle, in which the vanquished nation will not be overcome until the entire power of its people is broken, and even our people, even if we are the victors, will be utterly exhausted."

A true picture, but perhaps influenced by his uncle's, the elder Moltke's, dictum after 1870, that a future European war might be a seven years' war or it might last for twenty years.

It is intensely interesting to follow from Moltke's correspondence, the gradual collapse of his moral in August and September, 1914, under the load of responsibility which temperamentally he was unfitted to bear.

On 9th August he wrote :—

"It is heart-rending how little suspicion the Kaiser has of the seriousness of the situation. He has already a certain 'Hurrah-humour' that I hate like poison."

On 8th September :—

"I can hardly tell you how indescribably heavy the burden of responsibility has weighed on me in the last few days, and how it still weighs."

On 9th September :—

"It goes badly, the fighting on the east of Paris will end unfavourably for us. One of our armies must retire, the others must follow."

Change in German Supreme Command

The climax was now reached. The following description by Col. Bauer, Operations Section at O.H.L., shows the final collapse during the last stage of the Battle of the Marne :

"Panic seized the leaders of the army. Moltke completely collapsed. He sat with a white face gazing at the map, apathetic, a broken man. Gen. von Stein (Moltke's deputy) certainly declared, 'We must not lose our heads,' but he did not take charge. He himself was without confidence and expressed it by saying :—' We cannot tell how things will go.' Tappen (head of the operations section) did not consider it was his fault, he never lost his nerve, but that he ought to do something was not clear to him. 'We younger people could not get a hearing, but we agreed that something decisive must happen.' Gen. Sieger (in charge of ammunition supply) was informed ; he agreed with us and went to the Chief of the Military Cabinet. The result was that Falkenhayn took over command."

Ludendorff describes Moltke as :—

"A remarkable man. He had a keen grip of military affairs and could handle big situations with extraordinary mastery. But his temperament was not really resolute and his inclinations were more pacific than warlike."

Col. Bauer describes him as follows :—

"He was a highly educated, clever man, of blameless character. Despite an outward cold manner, he was sensitive, perhaps too much so. He had assumed his position as Chief of the General Staff in a spirit of absolute loyalty and subordination to his War Lord. He was, however, not a born leader, and at the commencement of the war was already a sick man. His handling of the army at critical periods was fateful."

Again :—" Moltke, on being informed of Prittwitz's decision to retire behind the Vistula in East Prussia, was terribly shocked, but would not give an energetic counter order. The junior staff, after hours of work at the telephone, got in direct communication with the Corps Commanders. All Corps considered the situation serious, but were opposed to any hasty retirement. The Staff then went to Gen. von Stein and finally to Moltke and with success. Prittwitz was relieved by Hindenburg, with Ludendorff as his C.G.S."

Moltke has been criticized as being a mere courtier, ignorant and untrained in the higher art of war. But, although he had not been at the German War College where their General Staff were trained, it seems clear that he was a clever man, a highly educated soldier, and had a pleasant character. His published correspondence shows him to have been a brilliant writer and a shrewd observer. Moreover, from his dealings with the Kaiser, it would appear that he held firm opinions, and had the courage of his convictions. On the other hand, he certainly failed as a commander in the field. Apart from any error in his plan of campaign, we have seen that he failed to control his armies or maintain a clear-cut plan. When great or rapid decisions had to be made, his will power failed him. His character was not cast in a sufficiently determined mould to stand the terrific strain which the control of a nation in arms must impose. In spite of Ludendorff's remarks, he certainly had not that wide outlook required to appreciate the big situations. He failed to get in personal touch with the armies and was content to sit in his headquarters far from the scene of the crisis on the Marne. Compare him with other great actors in that drama—Joffre, unmoved by the collapse of his whole war plan, set to work with ceaseless activity to reconstruct a fresh edifice, untiring he continually visited all his armies and imposed his wishes on his army commanders—Kitchener, with a lofty and broad outlook, foreseeing and organizing for a long war, but when the necessity arose, visiting the Front and enforcing the views of the Cabinet on the army in the field.

It must be admitted that Moltke, the chosen head of the renowned Great General Staff and leader of the greatest war machine in the world, lacked the strength of character and vision to fulfil his task.

OBSERVATIONS ON THE CAMPAIGN

1. The value of surprise. Although there was no great disparity in numbers between the Germans on the one hand and the French, British and Belgians on the other, the Germans obtained the initiative by the fact that their concentration of vast numbers on the right wing surprised the French High Command.

2. Vacillation between two plans and two objectives lost Moltke the initiative and ruined the German campaign. Having made a plan it is necessary to stick to it and concentrate all forces on its execution.

It would appear that Moltke might have brought about a tactical success, at least on the Marne, in spite of his initial

38 GERMAN STRATEGY IN THE GREAT WAR

vacillation, if he had taken determined steps to control his armies at any time between 30th August and perhaps 2nd September. He should have insisted on Kluck carrying out his rôle of right flank guard and getting into position on Bülow's right rear, thus obviating the gap which arose between them, and which was the immediate tactical cause of the retreat from the Marne. Further, he should never have permitted the fruitless attacks by Rupprecht of Bavaria on the Grand Couronné de Nancy which commenced on 4th September. Instead, three of Rupprecht's corps should have been railed round to Kluck and Bülow. This was possible, as a reference to the remarks on railways will show.

3. Detachments from the main operations are valueless unless they contain a greater number of the enemy. The Germans failed to do this in Lorraine. On the other hand, the Belgian Army at Antwerp and the garrison of Maubeuge (inferior French troops) kept six German divisions from the Battle of the Marne.

4. The necessity for headquarters to keep in touch with operations was borne out by the continual German failure to control their armies. They attempted to direct too many formations from too far in rear and with an inefficient signal service.

5. The necessity for direction as regards boundaries, frontages of operations, etc. Supreme Command's control was so loose that armies swung to and fro to each other's assistance, sometimes necessarily and sometimes unnecessarily and large gaps arose between formations.

6. The necessity for an efficient intelligence service was borne out throughout the operations on both German and French sides. The French did not appreciate until 23rd August that there were large German forces moving through Belgium north of the Meuse, although there were two whole armies there from 17th August. The Germans failed to appreciate the importance of the westerly move of the French forces between 23rd August and 5th September,

BATTLE OF THE MARNE 39

although the move was partially identified on 29th August.

7. *Railways*. The German War Plan involved rather a gamble as regards railways. It is certain that the successful advance of their right wing depended on getting rapid rail communication through Belgium. The Aachen—Liége line was vital to them and it contains a series of tunnels. The Nasproué tunnel is the first one inside Belgium. Although it contained, according to German evidence, four mine chambers, fully charged and ready to fire, the Belgians failed to fire the demolition charges. Instead, they endeavoured to block the tunnel by derailing seventeen locomotives in it. Had the mines been blown the tunnel would probably have been wrecked to such an extent that it would have been necessary to construct an avoiding line, a two months' task at least. Actually one line was in working order on 11th August and both tracks on 15th August owing to the slight damage done. Liége and the railway bridges over the Meuse were another vital link. In spite of these bridges being in the centre of a fortress, whereby the Belgian engineers should have had ample time to destroy them, the only damage done in Liége was the destruction of two small culverts, the removal of some point levers and the destruction of water towers. The great bridges over the Meuse were untouched. In consequence the Germans were actually handling trains in Liége Central Station on 15th August only 10 miles in rear of their leading troops. It is probable that the demolition of the Aachen—Liége tunnels and the Meuse bridges would have had a far more decisive effect on the German campaign than did the resistance of the Liége forts. Railhead was able to follow close in rear of Kluck's Army across Belgium. In fact, IX Reserve Corps moved by rail to observe Antwerp beginning to detrain at Louvain on 23rd August. Valenciennes was open to railway traffic on 29th August, Cambrai on 30th August, Roye and Chauny on 4th September, and Amiens and Compiègne on 9th September. (Map V.)

The First Army and the right of the Second Army were at no time more than 55 miles from railhead and were usually within 45 miles, a remarkable achievement by the German railway troops, but undoubtedly helped by inferior demolitions. Owing to very effective demolitions at Namur by the Belgians and at Maubeuge and Montmédy by the French, the Germans in the centre of their offensive wing were forced to operate far from railhead. Part of the Second, the Third, and probably Fourth Armies, when on the Marne, were as much as 100 miles from their railheads. The destruction of the Meuse bridge at Namur cut the very important lateral line Metz—Luxemburg—Libramont— Namur until 30th September, and other damage to this line prevented its use between Luxemburg and Namur up to 8th September. Tappen, the Director of Operations at O.H.L., has made this the German excuse for not reinforcing their right wing before the Battle of the Marne by transfers from the left. This can hardly be regarded as a serious excuse, for one must remember that the Germans had kept rolling-stock for three corps behind the Lorraine front since mobilization ended expressly for such a transfer and it is inconceivable that they should put sole reliance on a lateral railway so far forward in hostile territory. Moreover, when Moltke stopped the attacks between Verdun and Belfort and ordered troops to the West on 7th and 8th September, a cavalry division and two corps were actually moved from the Strassburg area via Saarbrucken—Trier— Aachen—Liége—Brussels—Mons—Cambrai to the Busigny —St. Quentin area, detrainment being completed on 15th September. Actually the leading Corps (XV) was in the line on the Aisne on 14th September, that is, within seven days of O.H.L. ordering the move. There would appear to be no transportation reason why this Corps should not have reached the Battle of the Marne before the crisis on the evening of 8th September if Moltke had issued orders even as late as 1st or 2nd September. Its arrival, followed rapidly

BATTLE OF THE MARNE   41

by a second corps and even a third corps, might have filled the gap between Bulow and Kluck and saved the day.

8. *The Value of Fortresses.* The Germans are reported to have lost 42,000 men before Liége, although they apparently did not lose much time. As we know, the German Armies received no drafts before the Marne. These losses were, therefore, a big item. Namur does not appear to have exerted any decisive influence, for it capitulated after only two days' bombardment. Antwerp contained two German corps from the end of August till 10th October, and thereby exerted a decisive influence on the Marne battle.

General Deguise, Commandant of Antwerp, has written since the war of the poor state of the defences which were not proof even against six-inch shells. Expenditure authorized in 1906 was deferred for political reasons and the defences were never brought up to date. In peace time the Belgian Minister for War had silenced military protests by declaring —" I am responsible to the people." On the approach of the Germans in 1914, as he stepped into his motor-car to make off, he said to General Deguise —" You are responsible for the defences."

Givet held up one division which only arrived at the Front during the Battle of the Marne. Maubeuge detained one corps from the Marne. If all these troops had been at the Marne there is little doubt that the gap between Bülow and Kluck could have been filled.

As regards the French eastern fortresses, their influence moulded the German plan of campaign before the war, and although few of the actual forts came into action, there is little doubt that the French would not have attempted the defence of the Verdun salient had it been unfortified. Its retention stretched the German armies to breaking-point.

Although new weapons of war may have nullified the existing type of fortress, there can be no doubt that permanent fortifications adapted to modern requirements will have an important influence in future wars.

THE RACE TO THE SEA. (MAP VI.)

The results of the Battle of the Marne were a withdrawal by the German right wing to the Aisne followed by attempts on both sides to outflank the other by an extension northwards. These movements culminated in the First Battle of Ypres which was a final attempt on the part of the Germans to obtain a decision in the West.

FIRST BATTLE OF YPRES

Falkenhayn's first big decision, to make a decisive attack at Ypres, was based on the following reasons: First, he was convinced that the Western Front must be stabilized and consolidated before attempting large operations in the east, he also thought that conditions of weather and ground in the winter were more favourable to continued operations in the west, and that the winter would soon check the Russians. The position in the west was far from safe or satisfactory for the Germans; their main line of communication for their western wing, the railway along the Meuse and Sambre to St. Quentin, was unprotected; the Belgian Army in Antwerp threatened their northern flank and was holding up two German corps who were watching Antwerp. The French railways were superior and facilitated movements of their troops to the north to outflank the Germans. But by means of a vigorous German offensive in the north there was still hope of seizing the Channel ports and thus seriously affecting the communications between England and France. The problem was to obtain the troops for this. Troops to extend the line to the sea to prevent envelopment by the enemy had already been on the move north from Alsace and Lorraine since 5th September. Now for the larger object of gaining the Channel ports and turning the French flank, a new Fourth Army was formed in the middle of October out of three of the divisions which had besieged and taken Antwerp together with four new army corps from Germany which were just complete and fit for service.

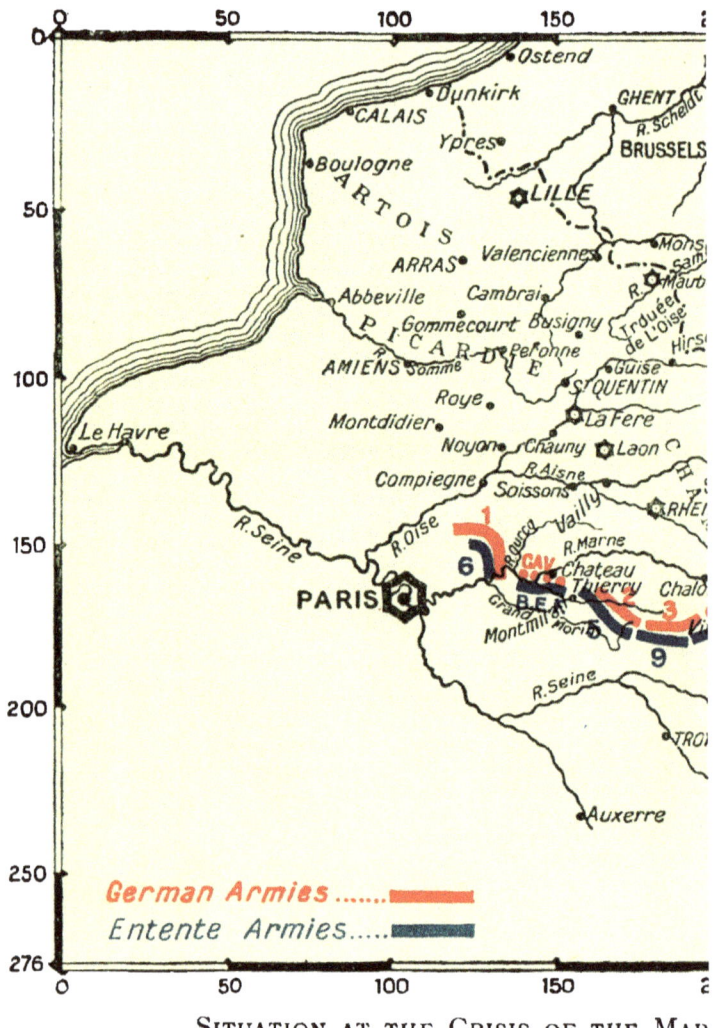

SITUATION AT THE CRISIS OF THE MARNE

MAP V

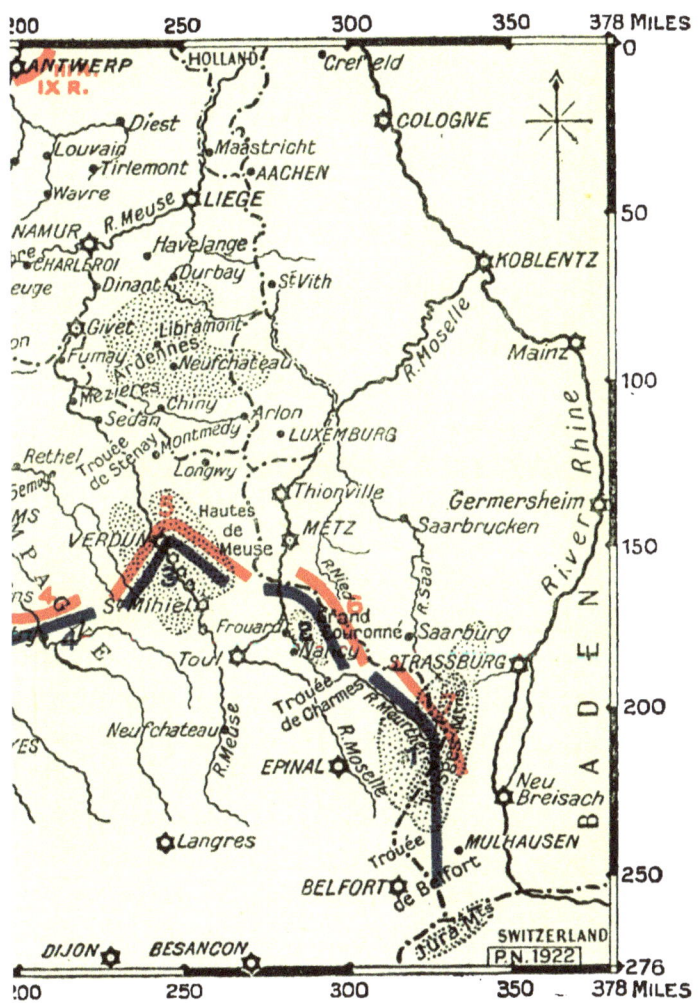

NE, 8TH TO 9TH SEPTEMBER, 1914

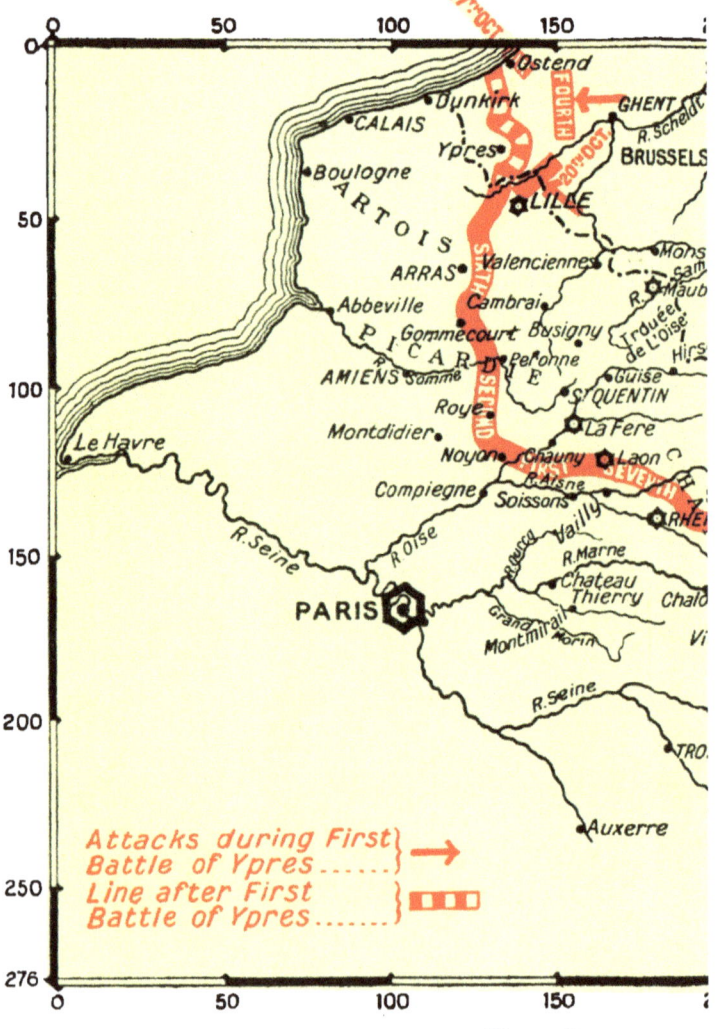

THE RACE TO T

MAP VI

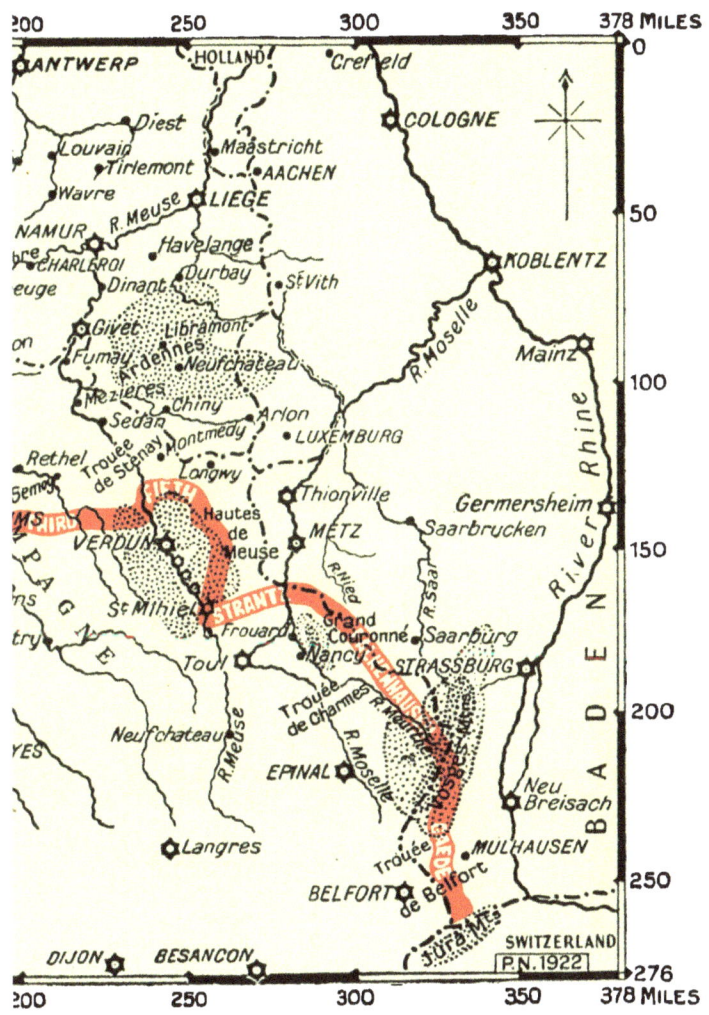

BATTLE OF THE MARNE 43

The possibility of a fresh break-through attack in Artois or Picardy or Champagne was considered as an alternative to the northern attack, but the number of troops and the means of transporting them would not allow of two concentrations, one to hold up the French and British enveloping movement in the north, and the other for an attack elsewhere.

The attack at Ypres by the Germans failed in its full objects of securing the Channel ports. The Germans claim it was of value in ensuring that they consolidated the Western Front. The Germans say that the failure was due to the Belgian inundations, to the difficulties of movement arising from the winter conditions which were not at first appreciated by the Germans, and to partial failure in higher command and junior leading in the new army corps owing to the officers being old and largely reserve of officers. Trench warfare thereafter set in on the Western Front. There was a further very good reason for the German failure: the stout heart and good fighting powers of the British Army.

CHAPTER VI
RUSSIAN PLAN OF CAMPAIGN

THE PLAN. (MAP VII.)

The Russians organized their military forces on mobilization into ten armies, the First to Ninth and the Army of the Caucasus. Roughly, four corps and two to three cavalry divisions were allotted to each army; the exact detail is in Appendix IV.

It is interesting to note that Russia, although backward in much of her military organization, was the only country who began the war with a higher organization than the army, that is the " Group of Armies." The Russians had three groups known as " fronts " and three independent armies in reserve.

The three fronts were the North-West Front, the South-West Front, and the Caucasus ; the first faced Germany, the second Austria, and the third Turkey.

The Grand Duke Nicholas was in supreme command with Headquarters at Baranovichi. His Chief of Staff was Yanushkevich, but the direction of operations appears to have been largely in the hands of Danilov, the General Quartermaster, corresponding to our Director of Military Operations.

The North-West Front under Jilinski at Byelostok consisted of two armies. The First Army (Rennenkampf) assembled on the east frontier of East Prussia and was intended to play a purely defensive rôle against Germany. The Second Army (Samsonov) originally assembled about Warsaw as a reserve with no allotted rôle. The Russians

RUSSIAN PLAN OF CAMPAIGN

had no intention whatever of fighting in Western Poland, which for many years had been left in as undeveloped a state as possible as regards railways and roads to prevent German incursions. All the strategic railways stopped at the Vistula or led south-west towards Galicia. At the beginning of the war both Rennenkampf and Samsonov had big military reputations; opinion was divided as to which was the more capable soldier, although it was thought Samsonov might have got out of touch with military ideas owing to four years' civil employment as Governor of Turkistan.

The South-West Front, under Ivanov at Rovno, contained four armies. The Fourth (Salza) and the Fifth (Plehve), deployed behind the Vistula in the Lyublin Government, had a defensive rôle to hold up the advance of the main Austrian forces which were known to be preparing to advance into Southern Poland. The Third Army (Ruzski) and the Eighth Army (Brusilov) formed the striking force of the whole Russian front and were intended to advance into Galicia to take the offensive against the communications of the Austrian Armies. The Russians, therefore, intended to execute a decisive operation against the Austrians involving the destruction, if possible, of the Austrian Armies, as soon as possible.

The Caucasus Front at this time was of course a peaceful front, and only two corps were kept there.

The Ninth Army (Letchitski) was to assemble at Petrograd for the defence of the coast and the capital. The Seventh Army at Odessa was to observe the Black Sea Coast.

The defensive rôle of the North-West Front was changed after mobilization with the sole object of helping the *Entente* in the West, and with this object an invasion of East Prussia was ordered by the First and Second Armies. To replace the Second Army at Warsaw, the Ninth was ordered forward from Petrograd, and the Sixth Army took its place in charge of the troops there.

46 GERMAN STRATEGY IN THE GREAT WAR

The Russian General Staff expected the Austrians to operate against them with three armies, total ten corps, from the line Tarnopol—Jaroslau towards the north-east. Actually the Austrians formed four armies, but the Russian forecast was in the main correct. Russia expected the Germans to confine themselves to the defensive with a force of about five corps on the east until after a decision in the west against France.

SITUATION IN THE EAST

In the east things at first went badly for the Germans. The Russians, contrary to expectations, had been in a position to invade East Prussia in addition to attacking and defeating the Austrian armies in Galicia. East Prussia was threatened from two sides, from the east by the Russian First Army under Rennenkampf, consisting of nine infantry and five cavalry divisions, and from the south-east by the Second Army (nine infantry and three cavalry divisions) under Samsonov. The II Russian Corps acted as a connecting link under Jilinski direct. Note that Ludendorff in his book grossly exaggerates the Russian strength and credited them with thirty-four divisions instead of twenty. For the protection of East Prussia, the Germans had their Eighth Army under General von Prittwitz, consisting of four Army Corps, actually nine active and reserve divisions, with certain Landwehr formations probably the equivalent of four more divisions. On the German-Polish frontier south of the Vistula the situation was stable with frontier guards holding the frontier. On 17th August Rennenkampf crossed the frontier, drove back the Germans and on 20th August achieved a strategic success at the Battle of Gumbinnen. By this date Rennenkampf had in places penetrated 50 miles into East Prussia and the seven or eight German divisions opposing him were in full retreat between the Masurian Lakes and the coast.

Further south about three or four German divisions were

being pressed very heavily about Hohenstein by Samsonov's Russians who crossed the frontier on 21st August. Samsonov was pushed forward before his concentration was completed. He was incomplete in transport and deficient of many units. Remember his army was really a reserve army. Also remember the wilderness of north-west Poland, no communications.

The Germans had already moved up to these two battlefronts nearly all available local troops. They could expect no slackening of the Russian pressure through Austrian assistance, as the latter had already been defeated in the opening battles east of Lemberg.

There is the problem that was directly facing Gen. von Prittwitz, the Eighth German Army Commander and indirectly German Supreme Command.

Prittwitz's solution was to decide to withdraw his army west of the Vistula between Thorn and Danzig and to hold the line of the river, leaving the Konigsberg garrison to hold out. His idea was that the reconquest of East Prussia would be easy with reinforcements from the west after a decision had been reached there. This scheme of withdrawal and reconquest was actually in accordance with Schlieffen's pre-war strategical conceptions. However, East Prussia was an important part of Germany, and Supreme Command did not approve of this plan. Moltke solved his part of the problem by appointing a new army commander and chief of staff, Hindenburg and Ludendorff, to the Eighth Army. These two took over the command on 23rd August, 1914, and by very skilful strategy working on interior lines, and by the good fighting of their troops they succeeded in destroying Samsonov's Army by 30th August.

They then turned on Rennenkampf's Nyeman Army with the bulk of the Eighth Army and with two additional corps which arrived from the Western Front, and within the next fortnight drove Rennenkampf completely out of East Prussia and across the river Nyeman.

The change in the German situation in the east shows

clearly the effect that a capable and determined commander can have on the course of events. Note once more Moltke's weakness in detaching troops from the west before his plan was completed there. No doubt political pressure was brought to bear by thousands of refugees from East Prussia who flocked to Berlin, but doubtless a stronger man might have resisted it. For it is to be noted that East Prussia was saved before these two corps from the west arrived.

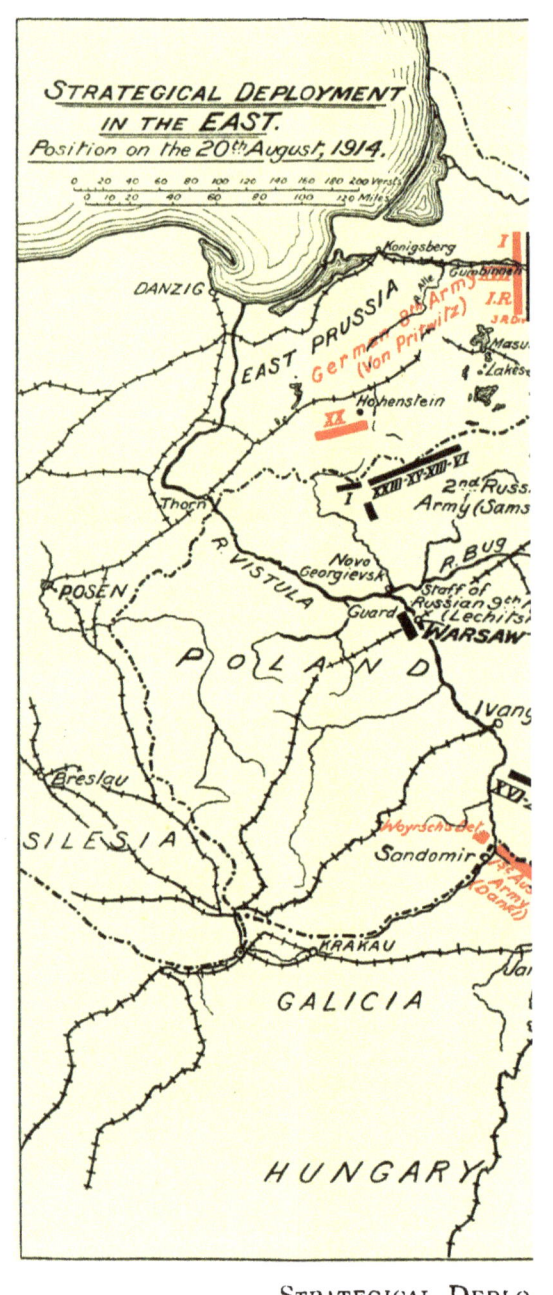

STRATEGICAL DEPLO

MAP VII

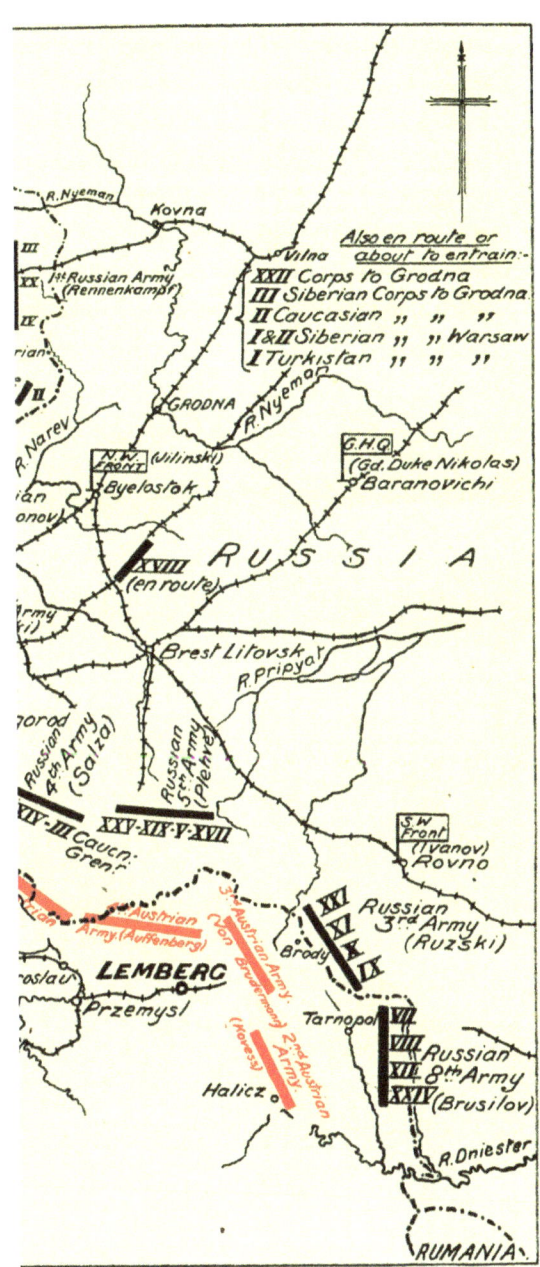

CHAPTER VII

BATTLES OF TANNENBERG AND THE MASURIAN LAKES

TANNENBERG. (MAP VIII.)

The situation confronting Hindenburg and Ludendorff when they took over command of the Eighth Army in East Prussia on 23rd August was as bad as it could be.

Rennenkampf's Nyeman Army, including II Corps, was advancing west from the line Goldap—Gumbinnen— Pilkallen on a front of some 40 miles with a total strength of eleven divisions and five cavalry divisions. The main body of the Eighth Army facing them, 3rd Reserve Division, I Reserve Corps, XVII Corps, I Corps and 1st Cavalry Division, was in retreat towards the outer defences of Konigsberg. Rennenkampf had suffered heavy losses in the battles nearer the frontier.

Samsonov's Narev Army of nine infantry and three cavalry divisions had reached the line Usdau—Waplitz and was opposed by the XX Corps with a Landwehr Brigade and some garrison troops from the Vistula fortresses. These German troops had had very severe fighting. The area of the Masurian Lakes, Nikolaiken—Lotzen—Lake Mauer, was well fortified with pill-boxes, trenches and wire and held by the Germans. At Lotzen there was a small "feste" (Fort Boyen) constructed in peace time.

The proposal to retire west of the Vistula had been abandoned by Eighth Army Headquarters and when Hindenburg and Ludendorff took over the intention was to hold the line of the river Passarge. This withdrawal would of course have permitted Rennenkampf and Samsonov to join hands and their superiority would have been overwhelming. Hitherto their two armies had been operating quite independently and with insufficient co-ordination.

The invasion of East Prussia in such strength by the Russians was certainly an unwelcome surprise. Reinforcements from the west could not be expected even under the most favourable conditions for some weeks. A purely defensive attitude until a decision was reached in the west had been the German intention in their pre-war plans, but this was based on mere theory worked out in war games. When it came to the pinch it was more than the Prussians could stand to have the important province of East Prussia, a hot-bed of Prussianism, overrun by the enemy. This civil pressure weighed heavily with German Supreme Command and undoubtedly also with Hindenburg and Ludendorff.

At all events they made their decision to attack the western Russian Army, Samsonov's, with all available forces, while holding off or rather merely observing Rennenkampf with a small force. In fact, they intended to act on interior lines against each of the separate Russian armies in turn, making the best use of the good communications of East Prussia, and taking advantage of the natural and artificial defences of the theatre of operations; first the line of Masurian Lakes, easily held, and second the outer defences of Konigsberg on the line of river Deime. This was a bold decision, one might almost call it rash, but it is not possible to tell how much Ludendorff was influenced by knowledge of the difficulties of Rennenkampf's rearward services in supply, reinforcements, etc., and of the fact that the Commander of the Russian North-West Army Group, Gen. Jilinsky at Warsaw, had hitherto failed completely to co-ordinate the action of the armies under him. Jilinsky's plan was to unite

TANNENBERG AND THE MASURIAN LAKES 51

his two armies about Allenstein and then clear East Prussia, but the mobility of the Germans was far greater than that of the Russians.

During the period 24th to 26th August the following moves took place in the Eighth German Army in accordance with Ludendorff's plan. I call it Ludendorff's plan as there is no doubt that from this time on Ludendorff's was the brain that conceived while Hindenburg was the figure-head on whom the responsibility was placed.

It would appear from a study of the literature on the German railways in the war that westerly moves by rail of 3rd Reserve Division and I Corps were commenced on 21st August under the orders of Prittwitz. The bulk of I Corps were to detrain at Graudenz on the Vistula. On 22nd August Ludendorff was at O.H.L. at Koblentz, passing through on his way to East Prussia. He made his first appreciation of the situation there and then, and fully realizing the high state of organization and good capacity of the East Prussian railways, he diverted I Corps by wire from Koblentz. The traffic was diverted from Marienburg on the Vistula to the Deutsch Eylau area, where detrainment was completed at eight detraining stations by the evening of 25th August. 3rd Reserve Division had detrained in the Allenstein area by the evening of 22nd August and then assembled west of Hohenstein, I Corps moved forward through Montowo.

Thus I Corps and 3rd Reserve Division were railed from the main body of Eighth Army to join Von Scholtz's hard-pressed XX Corps. XVII Corps and I Reserve Corps continued their retreat, but on 26th August moved sharply to the south to Bishofsburg and Seeburg. On the same day one cavalry brigade left the 1st Cavalry Division and moved south towards Sensburg. So from 27th to 30th August, the period during which the Battle of Tannenberg was raging, Rennenkampf's army had lost touch with the Germans and was only faced by weak detachments holding the area of the Masurian Lakes, two cavalry brigades from lake Mauer to river Pregal, and the Konigsberg garrison north of river Pregal. During this period Rennenkampf, pivoting on his II Corps at Angerburg, only advanced his other three corps to the line Nordenburg—Allenburg. Two cavalry divisions advanced on the south beyond Lotzen. Lotzen was threatened with bombardment and called on to surrender, but held out. Three cavalry divisions advanced on the north against Konigsberg, but were held up on the river Deime. Rennenkampf was completely out of touch with Samsonov, they had no direct communication, also Rennenkampf's slow progress was due to supply and communication difficulties. The German standard-gauge railways could not be used by Russian broad-gauge rolling-stock. But his army was only 50 miles from the battle and it is scarcely conceivable that he could not have sent considerable assistance if he had known the situation. Rennenkampf's ideas on how to pursue a beaten enemy or to press a retiring foe are shown by a remark made to one of his staff after the Battle of Gumbinnen who had gone to bed with his clothes on. He said, "You can take off your clothes now, the Germans are retiring."

The Russian wireless messages sent in clear were of great assistance to the Germans in showing the dispositions of the Russian troops. Samsonov's orders for the moves of his corps on 26th August were picked up by the Germans on the day of issue, the 25th. It is a notable fact that this use of wireless in clear by the Russians went on for about a year and of course made the task of the German Command in the east infinitely easier.

On 26th August the Russian Second Army had reached the following positions: VI Corps, with one cavalry division, on the right—Bishofsburg, XIII Corps between Passenheim and Allenstein, XV and part of XXIII Corps attacking Scholtz on the Hohenstein—Waplitz front, and the I Corps, with two cavalry divisions, on the left,

TANNENBERG AND THE MASURIAN LAKES 53

moving west through Soldau, and also in touch with I German Corps west of Usdau. In fact, the Russian Army was wheeling to its left, pivoting on the XXIII Corps.

Ludendorff's orders were for the southern group of the Eighth Army to attack on 27th August, against the front Usdau—Waplitz—Hohenstein, the I Corps to break through the Russian Army between their I and XXIII Corps in the direction of Neidenburg with the object of driving I Russian Corps south to Soldau and isolating and surrounding the main body of the Russian Second Army. The envelopment to be completed by the I Reserve Corps and XVII corps advancing south through Passenheim—Allenstein.

In addition to the corps mentioned, the mobile portions of the garrisons of Thorn, Kulm, Graudenz and Marienburg had been moved by rail to Lautenburg and Strasburg. They formed Von Muhlmann's force and were now guarding the right flank in touch with hostile cavalry; Von der Goltz's Landwehr Division was near Biesselen in the centre, having just arrived by rail from the duty of frontier guard on the Schleswig-Holstein frontier. This division was given the task of taking Hohenstein. A Landwehr Brigade was also co-operating with XVII Corps.

The attack on the south commenced at 4 a.m., 27th August, and after heavy fighting Usdau was captured in the afternoon by I Corps. The Russian I Corps was driven south to Soldau and I German Corps commenced its march on Neidenburg. The XX Corps, however, made no progress and was held up everywhere by the Russian XV Corps. By that evening I Reserve Corps and XVII Corps had reached the line Wartenburg—Mensguth, having defeated the Russian VI Corps on the evening of the previous day (26th) and driven it south. Von der Goltz's Division was approaching Hohenstein. On this day Samsonov was only worried by the fighting between Muhlen and Usdau. He was ignorant of the disaster to his VI Corps and the German threat from the north until the morning of 28th August. Actually the Russian VI Corps retreated after only a portion of one division had been seriously engaged, although the corps commander had clear orders to fight his way to Allenstein. The fact was, the Corps Headquarters had no communication with Army Headquarters and was ignorant of the general situation. Furthermore, one of its divisions bolted from the German heavy artillery fire.

Early on 28th, Neidenburg was taken by I Corps, but again no progress was made by XX Corps who, moreover, expected a hostile counter-attack. However, the situation improved in the afternoon, the northern flank of XX Corps making progress towards Waplitz and Hohenstein, and Von der Goltz entering Hohenstein after severe fighting with the Russian XIII Corps, which had moved during the day from Allenstein on Hohenstein. Meantime I Reserve and XVII Corps had again advanced to a line about 6 miles south-west of Passenheim—Allenstein. The Russian XIII Corps was thus getting driven into a ring with the other two Russian Corps.

On 29th August overwhelming success was made certain for the Germans by the closing of the circle along the line Muschaken—Willenburg by portions of I and XX Corps reaching the first place and portions of I and XVII the latter.

The Russian I Corps on the south joined in the battle again on 29th by attacking I German Corps at Neidenburg from the south. But after a critical period they were driven off.

Severe fighting took place on 30th August at Muschaken and the places where the Russians tried to break through the German ring, but these attempts never succeeded. Masses of Russian prisoners were captured on the 29th and succeeding days, the total being over 90,000. The Russian Second Army had been destroyed. The Germans claim to have killed, wounded and captured 170,000 Russians at a

TANNENBERG AND THE MASURIAN LAKES 55

cost of 15,000 casualties. Hindenburg and Ludendorff had their Army Headquarters throughout the battle behind the I and XX Corps and had practically no telephonic communication with the northern wing, i.e. I Reserve and XVII Corps, during 27th, 28th and 29th August. It was as much as they could do to get evening situations from these corps, on which they had to base general directions for the next day's fighting. But it should be remembered that Mackensen was on that flank, for at that time he commanded XVII Corps.

On the Russian side Samsonov moved on horseback on the morning of 28th August right up to XV Corps and was quite out of touch with his two flank corps throughout the battle. He sent all his wireless and signal apparatus back over the frontier with his baggage. All through the 29th August Samsonov with his Army Headquarters, now little more than a few mounted Staff Officers, accompanied XV Corps in their retreat through the woods north of Neidenburg. They could find no way through the encircling ring of the German Army. That night Samsonov kept saying to his staff that the disgrace of such a defeat was more than he could bear. At length he said :—" The Emperor trusted me. How can I face him after such a disaster ? " He went aside and his staff heard a shot. They saw him no more, and could not even find his body in the dark. The Army Staff escaped by walking 40 miles into Poland.

The Russian disaster was due to several causes. But first and foremost, the Russian Second Army, lacking equipment and communications and rear services, and commanded by such a man as Samsonov, was a very inferior instrument of war to the Eighth German Army handled by Hindenburg and Ludendorff. The Russian corps commanders were also very inferior and had small idea how to handle their corps or to co-operate with each other. They could do nothing without definite orders, which of course they never received. Three corps commanders, also Jilinski, were dismissed from their commands.

Jilinski, commanding the North-West Front, failed to appreciate the dangers attendant on operations on exterior lines with bad communications to the rear and no intercommunication between his armies, especially when faced by such an active mobile and highly-trained army as the Germans, who were operating in their own country, a country splendidly equipped with roads and railways. Lack of cooperation between Rennenkampf and Samsonov was another great factor in the Russian defeat. Firstly, Rennenkampf should never have allowed the Germans to disengage their whole army from his front. If there was any clear plan he should have pressed on at all costs to join Samsonov even with only a portion of his army if he could not supply all. Secondly, Jilinski should have kept Rennenkampf better informed of Samsonov's situation. The only orders Jilinski gave Rennenkampf were as follows—

On 26th August to send the reserve troops of XX Corps (two reserve divisions) to invest Konigsberg. Remainder to pursue towards the Vistula. The forward move only started on 27th, and then only with half the army, for Rennenkampf sent two whole corps to invest Konigsberg instead of the reserve troops of one corps.

On 27th Jilinski became aware of Samsonov's danger and ordered Rennenkampf to send II Corps to Passenheim and the left flank of First Army to advance, to co-operate. On 28th and 29th portions of II and IV Corps approached the line Bossau—Bischofstein and to the north. If only this move had been made two or three days earlier Samsonov might have been saved and the German left wing might have been crushed.

On 29th Jilinski ordered Rennenkampf by telegram to retreat, as Samsonov was already surrounded.

It would appear to be a mistake on Rennenkampf's part to detach half the First Army to Konigsberg. The garrison

TANNENBERG AND THE MASURIAN LAKES 57

could have been held in check with far less. Rennenkampf should have been ordered to move south-west with all his forces several days earlier than he did.

Jilinski failed in his plan, in rapid decision and issue of orders, and in furnishing information to his armies.

To consider the actual dispositions of the two opposing sides for battle. Samsonov had his five corps spread out on a front of 45 miles advancing with the bulk of his cavalry on his south-west flank. The Germans operated with two strong groups separated at the commencement of the fighting by some 20 to 30 miles, but which they succeeded in concentrating on the battlefield at the decisive time and place.

The result was that the Russian Army was split up into three separated groups by the first German attacks. The centre and largest group was completely destroyed while the flank groups were defeated and driven back into Russia.

MASURIAN LAKES. (MAP IX.)

At the end of August the Austro-Hungarian armies were in a critical position in Galicia, but before giving them any direct help it was essential for the Eighth Army to deal with Rennenkampf who, as a result of Tannenberg, had withdrawn his advanced troops, but apparently intended to stand and fight between river Pregel at Wehlau and lake Mauer.

The Eighth Army received at this time two corps and a cavalry division from the Western Front, and thus had six organized corps of two divisions each, together with 3rd Reserve Division, Von der Goltz's Landwehr Division, the Konigsberg garrison and Landwehr from the Vistula fortresses, a total of some sixteen or seventeen divisions with two cavalry divisions. Rennenkampf had eleven divisions and five cavalry divisions. It appears probable that the German formations were kept up to strength while the Russian divisions, according to Gen. Gourko's book, had received no drafts since they mobilized.

At the beginning of September the Eighth Army deployed

ready to advance on the line Willenburg—Ortelsburg—Seeburg—Wormditt. The newly-arrived Corps (XI and Guard Reserve) had been detrained on the northern flank.

Ludendorff's plan was to advance in three groups, making a frontal attack between lake Mauer and river Pregel with four corps, an enveloping attack issuing from the defiles of the Masurian Lakes via Lotzen and south of it with two corps and two cavalry divisions, and a flank guard of two independent divisions operating via Bialla and Lyck.

The Konigsberg garrison on the north to hold the line of the Deime and the Vistula fortress garrisons to defend the frontier about Soldau.

The advance began on 4th September, only four days after Tannenberg had ended. By the 7th the four northern corps had reached the Russian positions on the line Angerburg—Nordenburg—Gerdauen—Wehlau and commenced their attack next day. The attacks were not very successful and the Russians made heavy counter-attacks. This absorbed the only army reserve, a division of XX Corps west of lake Mauer which had been intended to strengthen the enveloping attack. East of Lotzen the fighting was severe on 8th and 9th September. However, the southern Corps (I) had evidently found the enemy's flank and on the 9th by moving northwards from Arys, it cleared the way for the cavalry and XVII Corps about Lotzen. Jilinski's chief of staff had advised Rennenkampf to withdraw, concentrate and threaten the German advance through the defiles of the lakes, but Rennenkampf said it would be bad for the troops to withdraw. Jilinski was ill. It was worse for the troops when the German blow fell.

The flank guard had been fighting from 3rd to 9th September on the Bialla—Lyck line against a superior enemy, but held them up, and finally drove them back to Osovets—Augustov—Suvalki, the two latter places being taken. This flank guard was of great importance as fresh Russian forces

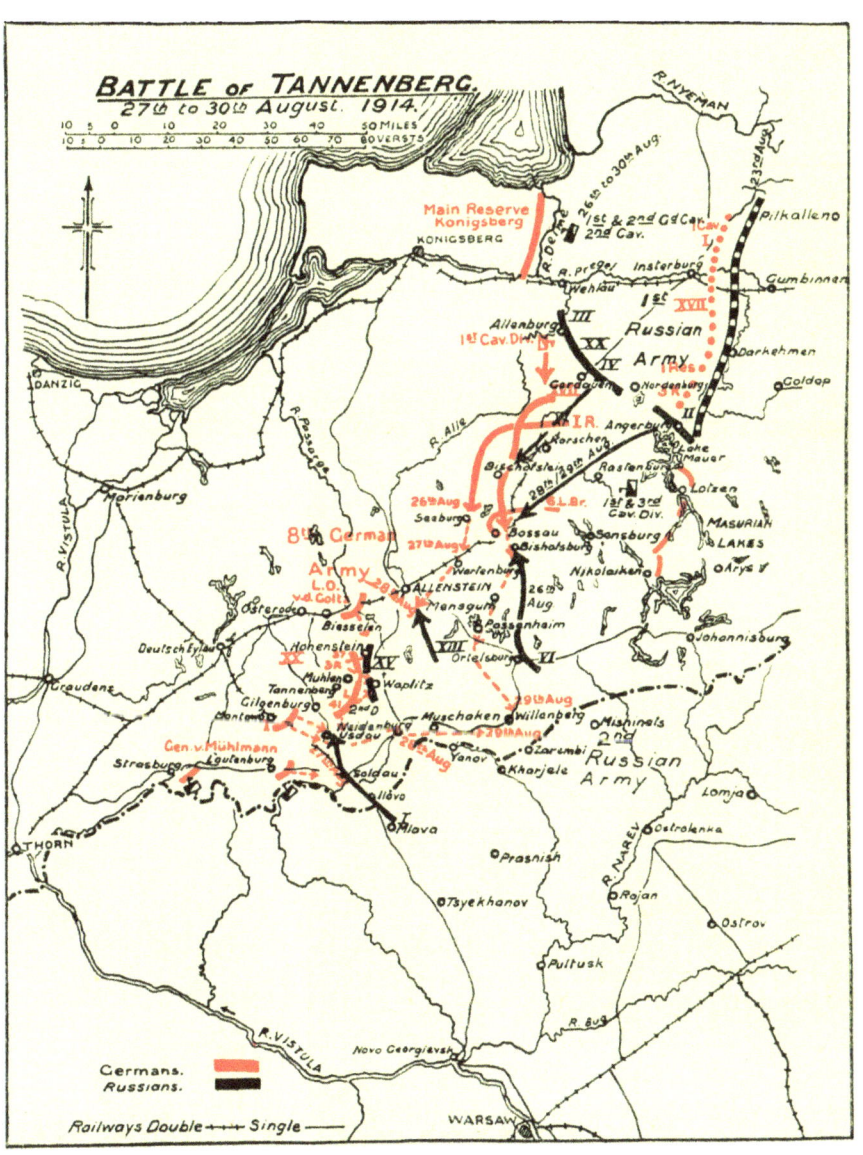

BATTLE OF TANNENBERG, 27TH TO 30TH AUGUST, 1914

TANNENBERG AND THE MASURIAN LAKES 59

from four to six divisions were assembling about Osovets and Augustov.

During the night 9th–10th September, the Russians began to evacuate their prepared positions at Gerdauen. The effect of the enveloping movement had begun to be felt.

A general advance of the Eighth Army was then ordered, the right wing being directed on Mariampol—Vishtinets and the cavalry divisions on to the Wirballen-Kovna road, so as to drive Rennenkampf back on to the river Nyeman. This advance developed into a pursuit of the Russians, a 60-miles' advance taking place in four days. The Russians became more and more disorganized as they approached the Nyeman and crossed the river almost a rabble.

The Russian version of this defeat which cost them 45,000 prisoners, is that the effect of the German cavalry, which appeared at first only in small bodies behind their southern flank, caused a panic. Further, Rennenkampf then lost control of his army and having first ordered an organized retreat, allowed it to become a rout.

On 13th September the battle was practically over and on that day the Germans had reached the following positions :—

Vistula fortress garrisons—Mlava.

Von der Goltz's Landwehr Division—held up by the fortifications of Osovets.

3rd Reserve Division, Augustov—Suvalki.

Two cavalry divisions and I Corps—Mariampol.

XVII Corps, XX Corps, XI Corps, I Reserve Corps, on the line Vishtinets—Wirballen—Vladislavov.

Konigsberg garrison—Tilsit.

Guard Reserve Corps had been withdrawn into reserve at Wehlau. The Eighth Army in their plans for this second battle made full use of operating on interior lines and turned to attack Rennenkampf with the least possible delay. In this case envelopment on one flank only was resorted to. The most dangerous flank for the enemy was selected, where his main communications by road and rail to Kovna could be cut. Advantage was taken of the country for this decisive enveloping attack to issue from the little known area of the lakes where the Russians expected no large forces. Once the Russian retreat commenced, the Germans pushed their pursuit relentlessly and thus reaped the greatest possible fruits of victory.

In the course of a fortnight the Eighth German Army had completely reversed the state of the war in East Prussia. Two numerically superior Russian Armies had been beaten, East Prussia freed of the enemy, and 135,000 prisoners taken, besides quantities of guns and stores. Some quarter of a million casualties had been inflicted on the Russians and, in fact, a quarter of the whole of the Russian Armies had been put out of action. The Russian armies had been fatally crippled and the *Entente* suffered from this till the end of the war.

There is this to be said for the Russians, that their rapid and unexpected advance into East Prussia with incomplete rear organization, had upset the German war plan from the start. It had been the direct cause of a diversion of force from the German armies fighting the Battle of the Marne, and had also absorbed large quantities of German munitions, a matter of no small account at that time. In fact, this relief on the Marne may have turned the whole course of the war.

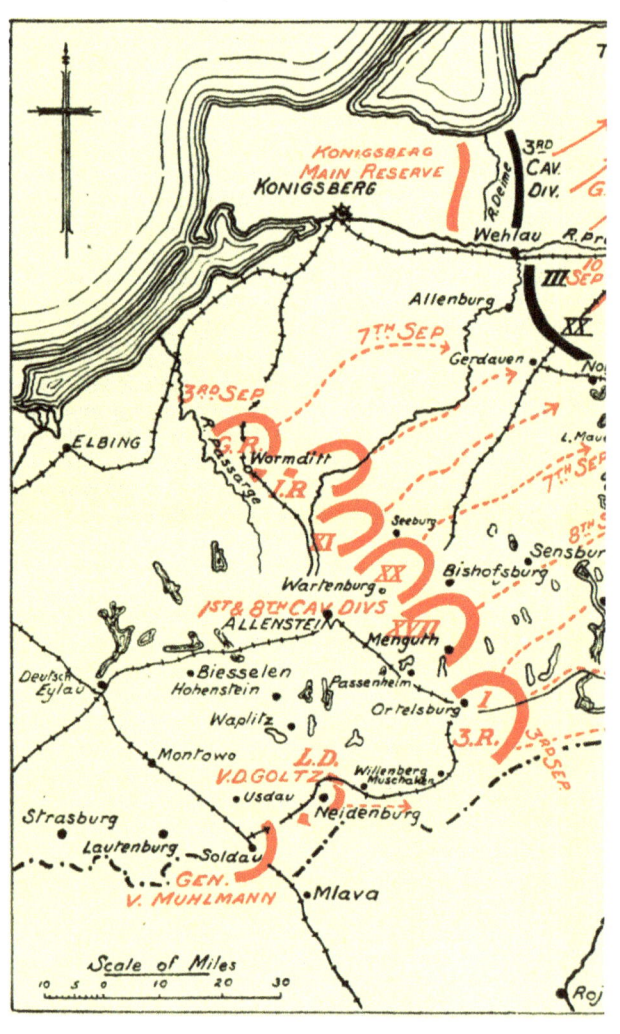

BATTLE OF THE MASURIAN LAKES

MAP IX

8TH TO 13TH SEPTEMBER, 1914

CHAPTER VIII

FIRST AND SECOND INVASIONS OF POLAND

FIRST INVASION OF POLAND, 1914. (MAP X.)

In the east by the middle of September the Russians had driven the defeated Austrian armies across the river San. The German successes in East Prussia were not of any direct effect in assisting the Austrians, distances were too great and Russian reinforcements were assembling in the north. Therefore, in order to try and rally the disorganized Austrians and to stave off the serious threat of an invasion of the vital territory of Upper Silesia, it was necessary to send German troops south to assist directly the Austrians. Further, the hopes of Turkey joining the Central Powers depended on stopping any further Russian successes. The alliance of Turkey and with it the permanent closing of the Dardanelles was essential to cripple Russia economically.

Accordingly, a new Ninth Army was formed under Hindenburg and Ludendorff consisting of some $5\frac{1}{2}$ corps. These troops commenced to entrain in the Lotzen area and the Konigsberg area on the night 16th–17th September and moved by two rail routes to the front Krakau—Krenzberg along the Polish frontier, where they were deployed ready to advance by 28th September. This move of $5\frac{1}{2}$ corps over a distance of between 400 and 500 miles required some 750 troop trains.

Only weak forces had been left in East Prussia.

The Austro-German advance commenced between 28th September and 4th October all along the line from the Carpathians northwards. By 12th October the German

Ninth Army was up to the Vistula and at the outskirts of Warsaw. They had only been opposed by a Russian cavalry corps of five cavalry divisions. But the Russians had made preparations on a vast scale for a counter-stroke and orders captured by the Germans gave away their plan, which was an advance in force across the Vistula from the San River to Warsaw with a strong enveloping attack from the north of Warsaw. In three weeks or less the Grand Duke Nicholas succeeded in moving three armies, Ninth, Fifth and Fourth, 100 miles north to the zone between Sandomir and Warsaw and in assembling a reconstituted Second Army at Warsaw. This re-grouping took place in safety behind the Vistula, covered by a mass of Russian cavalry west of the river.

THE RUSSIAN COUNTER-OFFENSIVE

The Russians held up the Austrian armies on the San River and on 18th October counter-attacked and began to drive them back. This, combined with pressure from the north-west of Warsaw and on the Austrians at Radom, forced the German Ninth Army to retreat. The whole line recoiled to the river Dunajec—river Nida—west of Lodz, where the Russian advance was temporarily checked by the very thorough destruction of roads and railways carried out by the German Ninth Army in their retreat from Poland. As an example of the Russian difficulties, for ten days their Ninth Army was supplied from the Vistula by horse transport over 120 miles of terrible road. Horses died in harness and men had to drag the guns. The situation was again very serious in the east. The Austrian Armies had by now lost 1,000 guns and 200,000 prisoners No reinforcements except for two cavalry divisions were yet available from the west, as Falkenhayn had determined to continue his attack at Ypres. In addition to the great Russian advance on the front from the Carpathians to Warsaw, attacks were developed

INVASIONS OF POLAND

in East Prussia by a newly-formed Russian Tenth Army. The German invasion was a bold move, but was undertaken with entirely inadequate forces, or else the Germans placed the Russian command and troops at a lower value than facts warranted.

At the beginning of November, Hindenburg became Commander-in-Chief in the East of all German troops, with Ludendorff as his Chief of General Staff.

The Grand Duke Nicholas intended to invade Silesia, and advance on Breslau with his Fifth, Fourth and Ninth Armies. The First and Second Armies were to guard the right flank while the Third and Eighth Armies in Galicia secured the left. This ambitious project failed through the difficulties of supply to the offensive group, the deficiency of communications in the whole army, and the slowness of the left flank guard to advance. The Russian armies stumbled slowly forward, while the more nimble Germans prepared a counter-stroke.

THE SECOND INVASION OF POLAND

The Commander-in-Chief in the East now decided on a bold move to throw back the Russians and possibly defeat them decisively. The plan, which was devised by Ludendorff, was to disengage the Ninth Army from the Chenstokov area and move it north to an area between Thorn and Posen, whence it could advance south-east with its left flank on the Vistula and attack the northern flank of the Russian main armies. Troops were also taken from the Eighth Army to assist. The transfer of the Ninth Army right across the front of the enemy involved another great railway operation, 800 troop trains were required, exclusive of ammunition and supply trains.

By seriously weakening the Eighth Army and the forces from Chenstokov to the river Varta, a force of $5\frac{1}{2}$ corps was concentrated for this blow under Gen. von Mackensen, who had been given command of the Ninth Army. Four corps

64 GERMAN STRATEGY IN THE GREAT WAR

were transferred from the west after the Ypres battle had ceased, but these arrived after Mackensen moved.

Mackensen's attack on 12th November surprised the Russians, for their intelligence service was inadequate and the Ninth German Army had been lost trace of for a fortnight. After severe and fluctuating fighting the Russians were driven back with the help of the reinforcements from the west, to the line river Nida—Skernevitsi junction by 12th December.

The details of this second invasion, culminating in a great battle round Lodz, are of extreme interest and form one of the most interesting operations on the Eastern Front.

The Battle of Lodz. (Map XI.)

By 10th November the German Ninth Army, under Mackensen, consisting of $5\frac{1}{2}$ corps and five cavalry divisions, was assembled between the Vistula and the Varta Rivers on the German-Polish frontier. Another corps was ready to co-operate further south (Posen and Breslau Corps).

This concentration was opposite the left of the Russian First Army, which was on a front of 100 miles with five corps, and the right of the Russian Second Army, which was more concentrated.

Ludendorff's plan was to crush the left of Russian First Army, rather isolated south of the Vistula, and then to envelope the right of the Russian Second Army and roll up the Russian battle-front.

Mackensen's advance began on 11th November and on 12th November he captured Vlotslavsk on the Vistula with 12,000 prisoners from V Siberian Corps. Rennenkampf passed VI Siberian and part of VI Corps to the south of the Vistula to block the German advance.

On 14th November II Corps (First Russian Army) and XXIII Corps (Second Russian Army) were attacked in overwhelming strength.

Schiedemann, commanding Second Russian Army, pro-

INVASIONS OF POLAND

ceeded to move his army so as to face north-east on the front Strikov—Lenchitsa and threaten a further German advance in flank. But the rapidity of the German moves nearly caused his troops to be defeated in detail.

On 15th and 16th November, the three corps of the First Russian Army south of the Vistula and the two northern corps of the Second Army were all heavily attacked and lost 25,000 prisoners.

The Germans were succeeding in splitting the First and Second Russian Armies, the latter being forced south-east to Lodz where its four corps were forced into a circle round the town.

Meantime Plehve's Fifth Russian Army was pushing forward all unknowing to the Silesian frontier. But on 17th November he retired under orders to a line due south of Lodz.

On 17th November, the Second Russian Army was in a critical position. It had been badly hammered by the Germans for the last three days, and now its right flank was completely turned, for a German cavalry division and $1\frac{1}{2}$ corps had got round right behind and to the south-east of Lodz. Three German corps were attacking frontally and driving the Russians back on to Lodz, while the Posen and Breslau Corps was threatening the Russian left flank from the south-west.

The Russian First Army could give no help, for its southern corps were retreating up the Vistula from the victorious German I Reserve Corps.

RUSSIAN COUNTER-MEASURES

However, the Russians succeeded by vigorous and well-timed counter-measures in saving their Second Army. The credit of these successful manœuvres must be given to Ruzski, now commanding the North-West Front, so far as their inception is concerned, and to Plehve, commanding the Fifth Russian Army, as regards their execution. If only Rennenkampf (First Russian Army) had carried out his share of Ruzski's plan, the tables would have been completely turned on the Germans and their enveloping wing would have been cut off and surrounded.

But, as we shall see, Rennenkampf failed to move in time.

Characters of the Russian Commanders

Ruzski, the commander of the Front, had been brilliantly successful as an army commander in August and September, but his health was bad and he only returned from sick leave to succeed Jilinski. He was a highly educated soldier, who knew how to use his staff, a thing many Russian generals failed in.

Plehve was an old man, bent and wizened, and also weak in health, but, in spite of this, he commanded an army with uniform success throughout the war, in 1915 and 1916 he was continually moved from front to front as he was one of the few Russian generals who could compete with the Germans. Plehve was of German origin and his character was quite different to the ordinary Russian, who is reputed to be merry, happy-go-lucky and careless. Plehve was dry, logical, unpopular, very exacting, but a man of iron will and unmoved in any emergency. He influenced his whole army to achieve great things. Sometimes his methods were unusual, when, for instance, later in the war he put sentries on the corps headquarters of his army and on the bridges over the Dvina to prevent them from moving back out of the Dvina bridgehead. It is interesting to note that Plehve's Chief of Staff was Miller, who later was with the British forces in North Russia after the revolution.

Rennenkampf had been a dashing cavalry leader in the Russo-Japanese War, but as the commander of a modern army he is described by Gen. Knox in his book as "an anachronism and a danger." His relations with his staff were a little strained, for one day he told his Chief of Staff

INVASIONS OF POLAND 67

to "take his snout away as he could not bear the sight of it any longer."

SUCCESS BY FIFTH RUSSIAN ARMY

Plehve was ordered north to assist the Second Russian Army. On 17th November he sent a division by rail to Skernevitsi, only one regiment got through when the line was cut by German cavalry. The rest of the division attacked the Germans at Tushin on 19th.

The rest of the Fifth Army marched north on 18th. On 18th and 19th the left of Second Army was secured by successful attacks by two of Plehve's corps west and south-west of Lodz. A part of this force then turned to face the more pressing danger from the Germans under Schaffer, commanding XXV German Reserve Corps, south of Lodz. They attacked the Germans on 22nd November from the west and drove them back. At this time these Germans were facing Lodz on the south and holding Rjgov, Tushin and Bendkov.

FAILURE OF RENNENKAMPF AND THE "LOVICH FORCE"

Meantime Rennenkampf had been ordered to act from the north. He despatched forces from Lovich on 20th November, and Skernevitsi on 21st. The latter had a division and a regiment and did nothing!

The Lovich Force had 3½ divisions, but it was hastily formed with no proper staff, transport, etc. Its commander was changed twice in thirty-six hours. It only moved 5 miles on 20th November. On 21st it reached roughly the line Strikov—Brezini and got in touch with the rear of Schaffer's German columns.

On 22nd the Lovich Force captured Strikov—Brezini and Kolyushki after heavy fighting and touch was obtained with the Second Russian Army at Lodz. II Russian Corps

68 GERMAN STRATEGY IN THE GREAT WAR

supported the Lovich Force at Strikov. It would have appeared that nothing could save Schaffer's German Force. At 7 p.m. Schaffer was ordered to retire by the German Ninth Army and to re-establish his lines of communication by driving back the Lovich Force. On 23rd November the centre columns of Lovich Force moved right through to the Second Russian Army near Lodz. The result was that the left of Lovich Force, one division (6th Siberian Division) was isolated west of Kolyushki. This division reported three German columns, estimated at three divisions, marching against it from the south. The 6th Siberian Division appealed for help to the Russian I Corps who had troops in Andrjespol, east of Lodz, only 4 miles from their flank. I Corps refused to move and on reference to Second Army nothing was done.

On 23rd, 6th Siberian Division fought successfully all day on the line Yanovka—Galkov. They captured German prisoners, who by this time were terribly depressed as they thought they were surrounded.

Early on 24th the German columns moving north worked round both flanks of the isolated 6th Siberian Division. The headquarters of Lovich Force were surprised in Brezini without any escort and escaped with difficulty to an armoured train at Kolyushki. It lost touch with the whole of its force and remained a helpless spectator of the destruction of 6th Siberian Division. The Russians at Andrjespol made a poor attempt about 9 a.m. to relieve their right (western) flank. A Russian cavalry division, supposed to guard their left (eastern) flank, retired at once. The 6th Siberian Division, assailed by three times its strength on front and both flanks, retired at 11 a.m., but finding Brezini in German hands, it broke up and only 1,500 men escaped to Skernevitsi.

Schaffer, XXV German Reserve Corps with 3rd Guard Division and two cavalry divisions not only made good his escape via Strikov to rejoin the Ninth German

INVASIONS OF POLAND

Army, but brought with him 16,000 prisoners and sixty-four captured guns.

THE GENERAL SITUATION END OF 1914

The Ninth German Army then received further reinforcements from the Western Front, released by the termination of the First Battle of Ypres. They advanced again and by 12th December had captured Lovich and Lodz. The Russians fell back to a line from Skernevitsi to the river Dunajec. The Russian offensive against Silesia was broken.

Meantime in the south the Austrians had held the Russians and in battles south-east of Krakau had driven them back across the river Dunajec. The winter season now called a halt in the operations and trench warfare ensued.

OBSERVATIONS

The value of a strategic retreat is exemplified by the German withdrawal after the first invasion of Poland. Roads and railways are vital to the operations of an advancing army. Their thorough destruction will stop an army of any size and allow the retreating force to disengage and even to regain the initiative.

To consider the strategy of the counter-offensive of the Grand Duke Nicholas in his method of advance to the frontier. He had not the necessary forces nor the communications to advance in deep columns on a continuous front as the Germans had done in Belgium in August. But he attempted to extend his First, Second, Fifth, Fourth and Ninth Armies right across the Polish salient on a front of over 250 miles. The result was a thin line everywhere, no reserves to meet eventualities, no power of manœuvre. The Germans, with their mobility and highly-organized communications, could strike him unawares anywhere and were almost certain to be able to break his thin front. The only counter open to the Russians was slow and ponderous side-stepping or retreat.

The Russians would surely have been better placed with their armies more concentrated, in greater depth on the front where they desired to get forward, i.e. Silesia and towards Breslau and with the intervals between armies or the flanks of their offensive group protected by the masses of cavalry which they had available, but of which they made little use.

Compare the bold plan for the second invasion of Poland with the conduct by Moltke of the first campaign in France. It required great courage and determination on the part of Hindenburg and Ludendorff to leave the Polish-German frontier almost unprotected during the move north of the Ninth Army. A commander who will take no risks will probably never win great victories.

The tactical situation in the Lodz battle and its kaleidoscopic changes are of course astounding. It would appear that the Germans attempted the operation with too small forces. If they could have delivered a more decisive blow on the south-west of Lodz and the Breslau Corps could have joined Schaffer at Rjgov, the Second Russian Army would have been destroyed.

The direction of the Lovich Force by Rennenkampf and his subordinate in immediate command was hopelessly inefficient. Right up to the morning of 24th November the smallest co-ordination would have entrapped the Germans. The closing of the gaps between Andrjespol—Yanovka and Galkov—Kolyushki was all that was needed.

The higher Russian Command also does not seem to have kept its subordinates informed, for Lovich Force knew nothing of Plehve's moves and that Schaffer was being attacked in rear at Rjgov and Tushin. Headquarters of North-West Front was 120 miles from the battle, too far for any useful direction.

The German cavalry must have kept their command well informed, they penetrated nearly to Petrokov. Mackensen at Ninth Army Headquarters was always in touch with

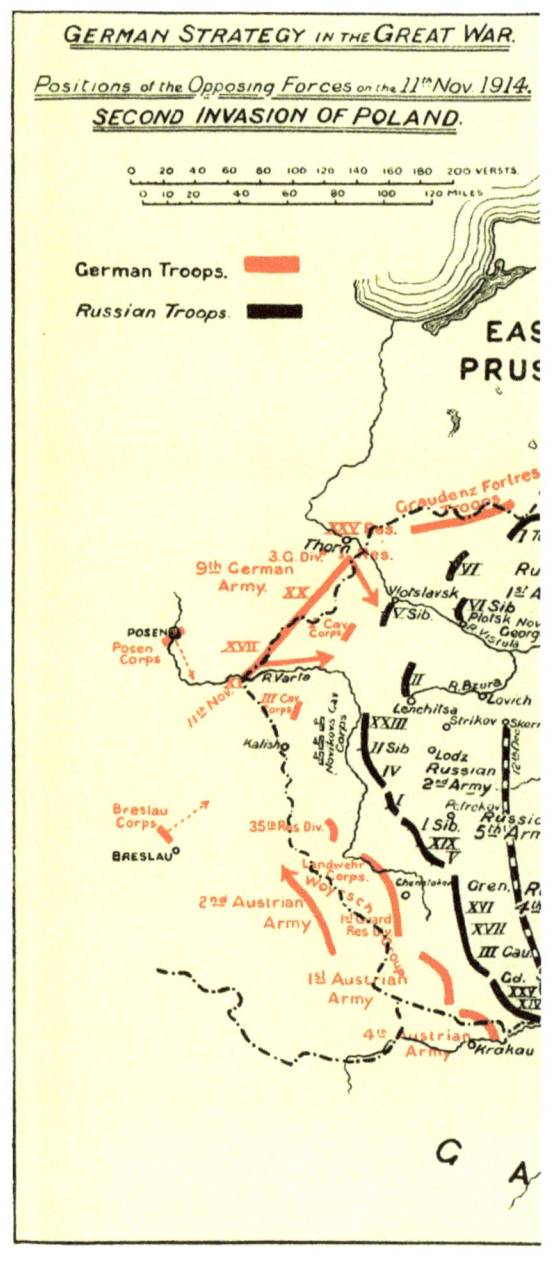

Second Invasi

MAP X

ON OF POLAND

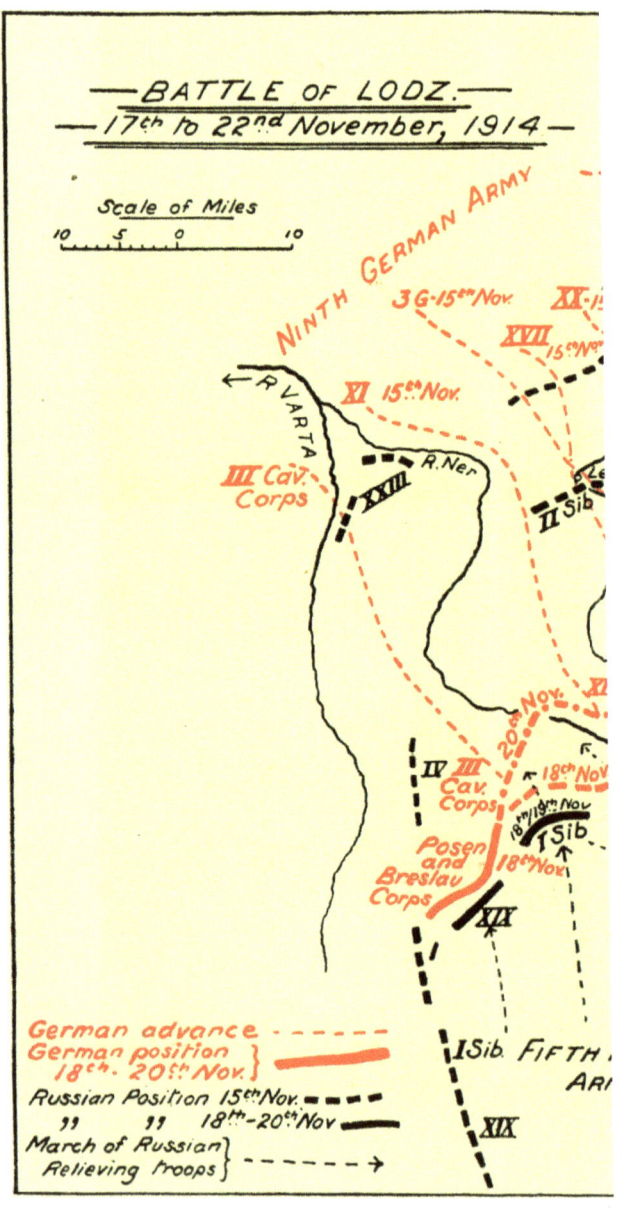

BATTLE OF LODZ, 17TH TO

MAP XI

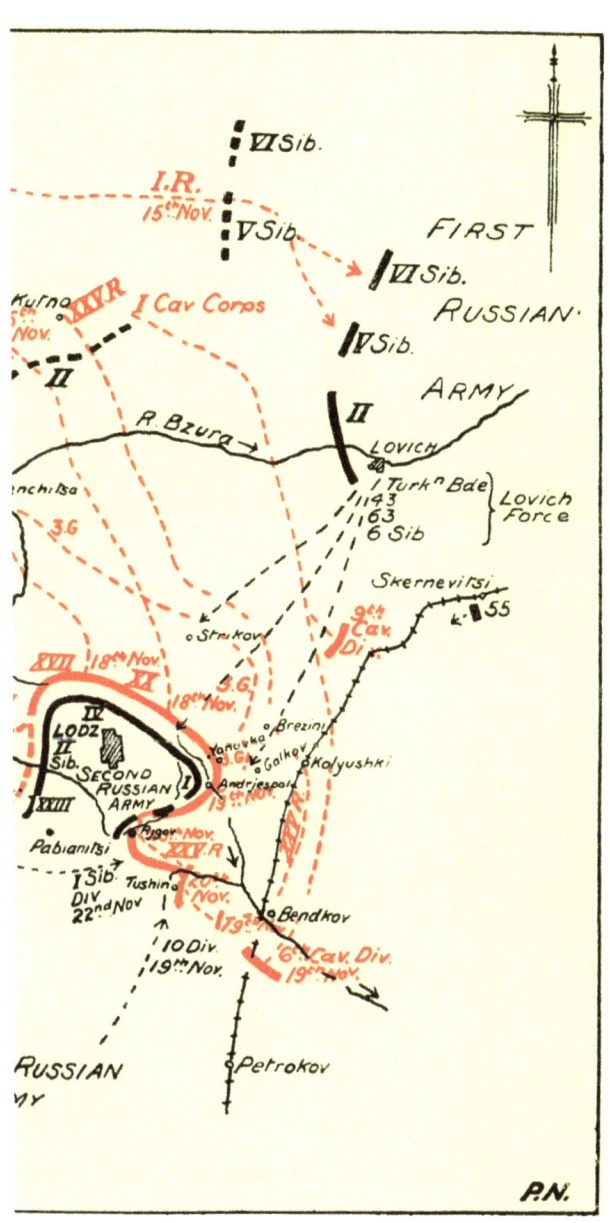

22ND NOVEMBER, 1914

INVASIONS OF POLAND

Schaffer and chose the last possible moment to order a retreat. With a more active enemy he might have been too late. The fog of war was, on the other hand, as black as night in the Russian Headquarters, and the only thing their cavalry appear to have achieved was the rapid retreat of a whole cavalry division from Galkov and the exposure of 6th Siberian Division's flank.

Both Germans and Russians in turn were within short distance of a great tactical success. In fact, the Russians were so optimistic that they ordered eighteen railway trains up to take the prisoners away!

These operations, if further details are ever available, will be of unique interest from the point of view of the psychology of command, and the strain on commanders' nerves. It is probable that Mackensen and Schaffer would come out of it with flying colours, for Schaffer's retreat was masterly and his orders must have been very rapid and clear. Whereas Schiedemann (Second Russian Army) was soon reduced to a state of inertia. Rennenkampf and his Lovich Force commanders (Slyusarenko, Shuvalov, and Vasiliev in turn) never had a grip of the situation. Plehve (Fifth Russian Army) was brilliant and he got his troops to carry out complicated and very long marches with great rapidity.

CHAPTER IX

"1915"

SITUATION AT THE BEGINNING OF 1915. (MAP XII.)

The Austrian Armies were being pressed by the Russians on the crest of the Carpathians early in 1915. The Austrian Supreme Command was anxious to relieve the situation there on the borders of Hungary and also to relieve the besieged fortress of Przemysl. They proposed to launch an attack from the southern part of their front and requested German Supreme Command to attack at the other extremity of the long Eastern Front, in the belief that a decisive success could be obtained thus against the Russians. The Headquarters of Commander-in-Chief in the East, i.e. Hindenburg and Ludendorff, were also strongly in favour of this scheme, considering that Russia might be finally defeated. There were four newly-formed corps in Germany now ready for use and both Austrian Supreme Command and the Commander-in-Chief in the East were anxious to use them on the East Front in an attack from East Prussia.

However, Falkenhayn, the Chief of the General Staff, was convinced that two operations so widely separated, 350 miles apart and conducted with the comparatively small forces available, could not achieve a decisive success. He also considered the Western Front the decisive theatre, and totally disagreed with the catchword going round in certain German quarters, that " the war would be won in the east." He considered that no decision in the east would affect the determination of France and England to fight on, and therefore determined that the Germans must first win victory in the west. So at the beginning of 1915 he determined to use the four new army corps in the west.

Falkenhayn wished the Austrians to give up their proposed offensive against Russia and use their troops to defeat Serbia finally, thus restoring their shattered prestige in the Balkans, shattered by their disastrous operations in Serbia in November and December, 1914, and open communications to the Middle East. He offered to carry out local attacks against the Russians in Poland to relieve the Carpathians Front.

However, the situation became so serious in the Carpathians that in the middle of January Austrian reserves on the Danube had to be sent there and German reserves from Poland also had to go to give direct support. This stopped any possibility of relief attacks by the Germans.

Falkenhayn then regarded the Austro-Hungarian armies as on the point of collapse. So he was forced to change his decisions regarding the new corps and sent them to the Eastern Front to carry out an attack from East Prussia while the Austrians did their best in the south, reinforced by the German troops (Southern German Army under Linsingen) already sent there, to clear the enemy from the frontier of Hungary.

At the beginning of February, 1915, the Austrians and Germans in the Carpathians attacked and recaptured most of the Bukovina, but they made little or no progress along the Carpathians to the north. No great success was obtained and Przemysl was not relieved. It fell on March 22nd.

WINTER BATTLE IN MASURIA. (SEE MAP NO. XII.)

In the north the Winter Battle in Masuria was started on 8th February by the Eighth and Tenth German Armies. The plan was to envelope the main Russian forces in East Prussia by strong attacks through Johannisburg—Raigrod on the south and through Vladislavov—Kalvariya on the north, that is, an enveloping attack on both flanks. The attacks surprised the Russians and a great tactical victory ensued, resulting in the destruction of the northern Russian Army, a portion of it being surrounded and forced to surrender in the Augustov forest. 110,000 prisoners were taken by the Germans. Owing to the severe weather, difficulties of communications, and the exhaustion of the troops, the operations came to a stop. East Prussia was again clear of the enemy. This success was followed by heavy Russian counter-attacks on the Polish Front against the Germans which were easily repulsed. But in the Carpathians the fighting again turned to a Russian offensive and at the end of March more Germans had to be sent to the northern Carpathians to support the wavering Austrians.

It appears that Falkenhayn was correct in his appreciation that nothing more than tactical successes could be gained by these operations.

It is interesting to note that Ludendorff in his book rather skims over the larger strategical aspect of these battles of February, 1915. Whereas it appears clear from Falkenhayn that Ludendorff was to a large extent the instigator of the combined Austrian and German plan. Throughout 1915 we shall see that Ludendorff hankered after a large enveloping movement from the eastern frontier of East Prussia.

From this time on Falkenhayn decided that if the Austrian Armies were to be used in offensive battles they must be directly supported by German troops, in fact the Germans would invariably have to act as the spearhead of the attack. He also made up his mind that with the limited forces available on the vast extent of Eastern Front, continuation of operations against the extreme flanks would not offer prospects of big successes. The point was that the enemy could not be tied down by frontal attacks sufficiently to allow strategical envelopment by the wings to succeed. The enemy could always retreat.

GREAT OFFENSIVE IN RUSSIA, 1915. (MAP XII.)

Austrian General Headquarters now, at the end of March, became so alarmed at the situation that they demanded from the Germans a reinforcement of ten German divisions. In addition, they thought that the entry into the war of both Italy and Rumania as enemies was imminent. The Serbians were also threatening to cross the Danube. In fact, the Austrians " had the wind up " all round. Falkenhayn, in preference to dispersing his reserves in purely defensive measures on the Austrian Front, now decided on an offensive campaign in Russia on the largest possible scale with the object of permanently destroying Russia's power of attack. Note that he did not hope to defeat finally the Russian nation and drive them out of the war. He wished to render the Eastern Front safe and passive so that he could again turn the main German Armies to the west.

Other factors which influenced this decision were that indications had been appearing amongst the Russians of serious shortage of trained reinforcements and also shortage of rifles and munitions. As a matter of fact, the Russian expenditure of shells had averaged *45,000 a day* since the beginning of the war, while their home production was only *35,000 rounds a month*. The whole of their mobilization reserve had gone and they were very slow to place orders abroad. At the beginning of 1915 the establishment of the forty-seven corps on the front should have been 2,200,000 combatants. The total strength on the front was only 1,200,000. There were no trained reserves available. Rifles also were deficient. Drafts came up unarmed and waited to be equipped from dead men.

It also became clear to Falkenhayn that the French and British offensives in the west which commenced seriously in March, could be held in check with less forces than were then on the Western Front. Until the March battles on the west, that is, in the Champagne and at Neuve Chapelle, had

76 GERMAN STRATEGY IN THE GREAT WAR

been fought and the defence had been successful, Falkenhayn dared not weaken that front. After those attacks he had a fairly clear idea of what the German troops could achieve in defence.

Falkenhayn's reasons against enveloping operations have already been given ; he decided on a break-through attack, and after considering communications for concentration and supply, and obstacles to be faced in the advance, the front between the northern Carpathians (Beskiden Mountains) and the upper Vistula was chosen. Also large Russian forces had recently been withdrawn from there for their Carpathian offensive. Falkenhayn attached such importance to secrecy that he did not even inform Austrian Supreme Command of his decision until the middle of April, when the German troops were already entrained for the move to their concentration area. In spite of this, the Russians received some warning, but did not act upon it in time. On 24th April successful attacks were carried out from East Prussia as a diversion. They drew considerable Russian reinforcements north.

On 2nd May the great attack was begun by the Eleventh German Army under Mackensen on the river Dunajec between Gorlice and Tarnow. This army was composed mainly of formations from the Western Front. Very great success was achieved, and after a month's operations Przemysl and the river San were reached, and the Russians were retreating on a front of 250 miles.

During May there were big efforts on the Western Front in the way of relief offensives by the English between Bethune and Armentières and by the French between Arras and Lens. These attacks were all held. On 24th May, Italy declared war against Austria. Austria wished to divert forces from the Galician offensive to crush Italy at once, but Falkenhayn would under no circumstances agree to this. He insisted on a policy of defence in the mountains and on the Isonzo, and to assist in this he consented to relieve Austrian troops on the Danube with new German formations. These German formations were then suitably placed for use against Rumania or Serbia as required.

To revert to the Galician operations. These had practically come to a standstill on river San owing to heavy Russian reinforcements coming up. If the situation remained like this, prospects were bad. Russian counter-attacks had already commenced and the Austrian Armies would disintegrate under them. It was essential to continue to attack and defeat the Russians. No other sector of the Eastern Front offered such good prospects as the river San. By continuing the advance here first eastwards and then northwards there were prospects of outflanking and enveloping the whole Russian-Polish Front. The Russians had no further prepared positions in this sector. A transfer of the attacking armies to another part of the front would not offer such good prospects and would also cause delay in which the Russians could reorganize.

Therefore, at the end of May, the Germans brought all possible reinforcements to Galicia by thinning out the remainder of the Eastern Front, by drawing in the new formations from their training-grounds on the Danube, and by transferring $2\frac{1}{2}$ more divisions from the west, reducing their reserves there to a dangerous minimum. In this way $6\frac{1}{2}$ fresh divisions were concentrated.

In the fresh attacks success was achieved, although no great enveloping movement ensued owing to the failure of the Austrians south of the river Stryj. Lemberg was taken on 22nd June.

These events led to certain immediate advantages to the Central Powers; as the threat to Hungary was removed, Austria could send sufficient reinforcements to the Italian Front; Turkey was relieved from an attack on the Bosphorus for which a Russian army had been prepared at Odessa; finally, the pacification of Rumania's hostile intentions and the resumption of negotiations with Bulgaria ensued.

Falkenhayn now considered the possibility of continuing the attacks. The reserves on the Western Front had become so exhausted that he had to return four divisions from Galicia to the west, and, moreover, indications pointed to great French and British attacks at a later period, about September, which would certainly involve further transfers. He therefore determined to continue operations with a limited objective. This was in contradiction to Ludendorff's views. The latter now advocated a decisive attack on Kovna and north of it in the direction of Vilna and Minsk in order to cut off all the Russian forces in the Polish salient.

However, Falkenhayn insisted on his plan of continuing his main attack in the south, but this time to attack in a northerly direction towards Brest Litovsk. As the Russians had strong forces on this flank of the Polish salient, it was necessary to assist by attacks elsewhere. The Commander-in-Chief in the East, Hindenburg, was therefore ordered to co-operate by attacking on the river Narev sector, and was not to attack north of Kovna until these attacks had succeeded.

The attacks in the middle of July were successful both north and south, but necessitated the transfer of two divisions back from the west.

By the middle of August the Russians had been driven out of the Polish salient, but they had escaped without being surrounded as the Germans had hoped.

In this connection there was some acrimonious correspondence between German Supreme Command (Falkenhayn) and the Commander-in-Chief in the East (Hindenburg and Ludendorff) as to this failure. Hindenburg insisted that he would have succeeded in cutting the Russians off if he had attacked in strength at Kovna.

Falkenhayn replied that if the maximum force available

had been used by Hindenburg in the Narev operations they would have succeeded in penetrating sufficiently far to the south-east. It was a fact that Hindenburg had kept from two to four divisions up his sleeve during the Narev attacks, ready for his later Kovna operations.

At all events, in the middle of August, Falkenhayn decided to stop any further major operations in the east for the following reasons : there were now no further prospects of big strategical success ; he wished to prepare the campaign against Serbia which he had been working for all this year and Bulgaria was now on the point of coming in ; the storm cloud in the west was on the point of bursting in Champagne and Artois. Transfers of troops were immediately necessary.

There were further isolated attacks by the Commander-in-Chief in the East, on the north, and by the Austrians in the south, and by the end of September the line ran from Czernowitz—Tarnopol—Pinsk—Baranovichi—Dvinsk—west of Riga.

By the end of 1915 the Russian Armies had been reduced by wastage to a total of 650,000 rifles, to defend a front now 1,000 miles long. Divisions were far below establishment, the depots had been drained of drafts, and no more rifles were available to arm recruits.

Defensive in the West

The great attacks in the west on 25th September, 1915, tested the German Army almost to the limit, all the general reserves on the west were absorbed on the first day, and the Third German Army on the Champagne front very nearly commenced a general retreat, but was stopped by Supreme Command, which arrived on the Western Front from the east on 25th September. Divisions from Russia were absorbed as fast as they arrived.

The German Front held firm and by the middle of October the fighting died down.

CAMPAIGN IN SERBIA

Meantime the campaign against Serbia was commenced under the direction of Field-Marshal von Mackensen with the Eleventh German Army of seven divisions, Third Austro-Hungarian Army of four Austrian and three German divisions, and six Bulgarian divisions (equivalent in infantry to twelve German divisions).

This overwhelming force attacked the Serbians from two sides, north and east, and rapidly overran the country. The operations started on 6th October, 1915, and by 25th November practically the whole of Serbia was overrun and the Serbian Army dispersed. This had the effect of opening up communication between Germany and Turkey. Munitions could be sent, which made a great difference to Turkey's fighting power.

OBSERVATIONS

A tactical success will not achieve great results without a sound strategical plan. The distance apart of the flanks and the lack of force rendered the operations in Masuria and the Carpathians in February, 1915, barren of strategical results.

The proper use of reserves by Falkenhayn in April and May, 1915, is worthy of note. He used them for a decisive blow instead of dribbling them into action defensively as requested by the Austrians.

The battle on river Dunajec by Mackensen's Army demonstrates that in modern war " break-through " attacks may have decisive strategic results, although most of the experience of the last war points to envelopment.

Loyalty on the part of subordinate commanders to the plans and orders of the Higher Command is essential. Failure in this respect on the part of Hindenburg and Ludendorff may have allowed the Russians to escape disaster in Poland.

MAP XII

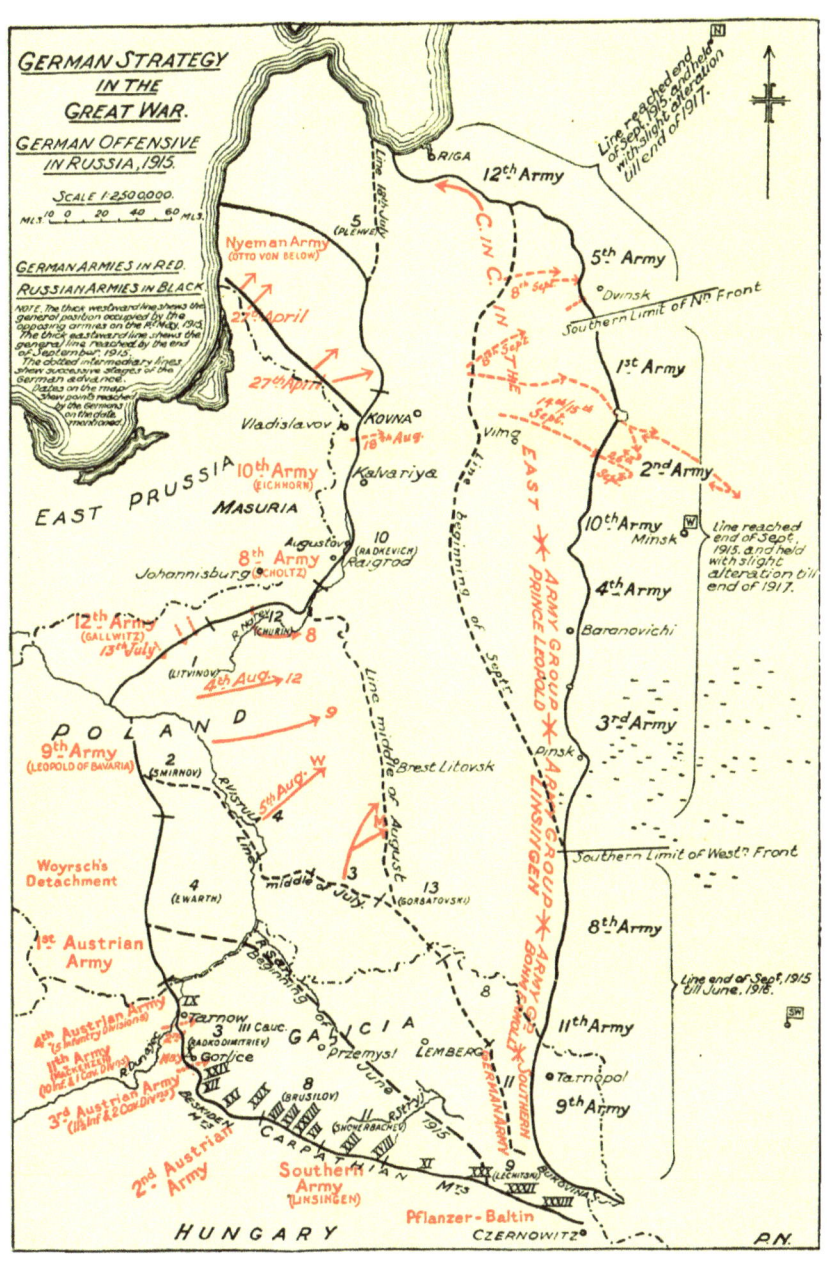

GERMAN OFFENSIVE IN RUSSIA, 1915

CHAPTER X

"1916"

SITUATION AT THE BEGINNING OF 1916

The general situation as visualized by Falkenhayn in the winter of 1915–16 was as follows :—

France had been weakened almost to the last limit. The offensive power of the Russian Army was shattered. Serbia had been destroyed.

Italy was by this time disillusioned in her hopes of rapidly gaining her war aims.

England's determination and her hold on her allies was the chief menace.

In coming to a decision as to future operations, consider first the possibility of a blow at England on land. A blow at her in the east would be of no value, as it would not affect the result of the war even though it intensified England's difficulties in the Mohammedan world.

In the European theatre the problem was very difficult. The only objective worth while striving for would be to drive the English into the sea and the French south of the Somme. Even if this was successful, a further operation would be necessary, as the French Army would still be intact. The only means of achieving such a task would be by a breakthrough attack in mass, with a minimum strength of thirty divisions in the first attack followed by many others.

Lessons from the French and British attacks in 1915 held out no prospect of success against an enemy equally well armed and of similar numerical strength. The salients made by such attacks, exposed to flanking fire, would become mere slaughter-houses in which the attacking troops would be decimated.

As the total German reserves on the west would only amount to twenty-five or twenty-six divisions, even after reducing other fronts to a dangerous extent, such operations were not considered possible.

But if England's allies could be put out of the war, England, left alone, would probably give up.

It was necessary to employ every possible weapon that could strike at England, especially submarine warfare.

Now as regards which ally to attack. Italy's desertion alone would make no serious impression on England. Italy's military achievements were so small and she was so firmly in England's grip that it was not possible to agree to Austria's desire for a decisive attack on Italy. Besides, in any case, internal difficulties might drive Italy out of the war without further fighting. In Russia the same internal difficulties might compel her to give in, even if there was no revolution in the grand style. In the meantime she was not likely to revive her military reputation. German forces were not available for a decisive operation. Therefore a fresh attack on Russia was excluded.

There remained France. Positive military reasoning agreed with the above negative reasoning. A break-through attack was not necessary. The result of making France reach the breaking-point could probably be achieved with limited resources. There were certain objectives close to the French Front for the retention of which France must throw in her last man. The French Army would bleed to death and the moral effect on France if the objective was reached would be enormous.

Such an offensive was safest for Germany, as she could accelerate it or break it off at will.

Objectives :—Verdun or Belfort. Verdun is within 12 miles of the German main lateral railway and therefore a standing threat to Germany. It would, therefore, be most advantageous to make Verdun the objective.

VERDUN

The attack on Verdun commenced on 22nd February and was carried on continuously until 11th July, when the last big attack took place there. The Germans only succeeded in advancing a maximum depth of 4 or 5 miles.

Falkenhayn had misjudged the French determination to hold on, and the strength of the Franco-British *Entente* or alliance.

RUSSIAN OFFENSIVE, MARCH, 1916. (MAP XIV.)

During the winter of 1915–16 the Russian General Headquarters, now under the Czar with Alexyiev as his Chief of General Staff, decided to make a great offensive from the Western Front with subsidiary operations on the North Front. The South-West Front was to remain passive. It is not clear why the offensive was to take place up in the north against the Germans, for hitherto the Russians had consistently failed against the Germans, and just as consistently succeeded against the Austrians.

The main effort was to be made by the Second Russian Army on each side of lake Narotch, with a strength of ten corps and a cavalry corps, with the object of breaking through and moving on Ponevjej, 100 miles to the west where they were to be joined by the Fifth Army who were attacking on a smaller scale from the Jacobstadt bridgehead in the north —an ambitious project. Smirnov, the commander of the Second Army, went sick just before the battle. There were four corps at hand as a reserve in the hands of the Army Group Commander.

The Germans had warning as usual and moved the equivalent of some five divisions to the threatened front.

The offensive commenced on 18th March, meantime a thaw had set in on 17th March, rendering the movement of all transport practically impossible. Why the Russians chose this time of year is inconceivable. Movement is possible on frozen ground in January and February, or on dried ground in June and onwards, but the annual thaw in March and April renders roads and open country alike impassable. Possibly help to the French at Verdun was the chivalrous reason.

After ten days, by 27th March, part of the offensive front had become a lake and operations had to cease. Nowhere was ground permanently gained, the greatest depth of penetration was only 2,000 yards.

The Russians lost between 100,000 and 150,000 men in this latter part of March in these operations. Generally speaking, the artillery bombardments were quite inadequate and the artillery failed to support the infantry in their advance. Desertion was rife from the infantry. After the thaw it froze again and on the morning of 22nd March, 300 men of one division were frozen to death and had to be hacked out of the ice where they lay.

No wonder Falkenhayn characterizes these Russian efforts as bloody sacrifices rather than attacks.

Meantime the Germans thought the southern part of the Eastern Front held by the Austrians, quite safe, for all the Russian reserves were in the north.

The Russians next turned to preparing a great offensive at Molodechno (south of the March offensive), to take place early in July, again under the command of the Western Front which, by June 1st, had five armies with fifty-eight divisions, while the Northern Front had thirty-eight divisions, and the much longer South-West Front also had only thirty-eight divisions. South of river Pripyat, i.e. opposite South-West Front, there were only two German divisions. North of the river Pripyat there were only two Austrian divisions.

Brusilov's Offensive

In March, 1916, Gen. Brusilov had been promoted from the Eighth Army, with which he had been consistently successful, to command the South-West Front. On 20th April he ordered all his armies to make plans for an offensive with only the resources then in their armies. Sectors where penetration could be achieved with small resources were to be selected and secrecy was enjoined.

In the middle of May the Austrians embarked on an adventure of their own devising in Italy contrary to the very strongly expressed wishes of German Supreme Command, who by this time had no faith in the Austrians undertaking any operations unsupported by German troops.

The Austrians reduced their strength opposite the Russian South-West Front in order to attack the Italians in Tirol. Their offensive had a certain success, but Italian counter-attacks finally drove them back practically to their original line.

It is believed that the King of Italy had made a personal appeal to the Czar for help. Brusilov was at all events asked if he could attack, and he replied, " as well now as some weeks later," which was his original intention.

His offensive was therefore launched on 4th June merely as a demonstration with local resources to keep the Austrians occupied on the Russian Front. Unfortunately there were no reserves within reach to exploit success, for Brusilov's attack came like a thunderbolt on the Austrians, whose front crumbled and broke from the Pripyat to the Carpathians.

The extraordinary contrast between German, Russian and Austrian troops is well brought out in these operations. The Austrian Army was practically only saved from dissolution, in spite of Brusilov's lack of reserves, by the presence of two German divisions in Linsingen's mixed German and Austrian Army just south of the Pripyat. This limited the penetration on the north and prevented expansion of the break. Also one German division in Bothmer's southern German Army in the centre of the Austrian Front prevented one of Brusilov's armies, the Eleventh, from advancing at all in the first attack, for the sector they chose to attack was apparently held by Germans.

Brusilov's offensive was far more carefully prepared than the main Russian efforts in the north. Brusilov's immediate success completely upset all the calculations of Russian General Headquarters.

The Molodechno offensive was now abandoned and attempts made to pour troops to the South-West Front. It was, however, a race between the Russian railways and the German and Austrian railways, for the Germans began to send troops to the broken front from all theatres. Needless to say, the Russian railways did not win.

There was one more attack on the West Front at Baranovichi, made to hold the Germans in the north. Launched without due preparation, it failed with heavy loss, 80,000 Russian casualties in twelve days.

Brusilov's attacks continued in a second phase in July, when there were further great successes at Brody and Stanislau. The Eleventh Russian Army captured 40,000 prisoners at Brody alone in a very finely conceived operation. The Germans again saved the situation.

By the middle of August the Russians had taken 360,000 prisoners and 400 guns. The final check in the offensive at this time was entirely due to the arrival of adequate German reinforcements. It must be remembered that this great success was achieved with equipment and guns that would have been laughed at on the Western Front, and therefore the Russians paid the price in blood, for their losses in the first twenty-seven days were 375,000 and by the end of October more than a million on the South-West Front.

On 27th August Rumania declared war on the Central Powers.

CAVALRY IN BRUSILOV'S OFFENSIVE

The use of the Russian cavalry during these operations is interesting, especially as Gen. Knox, then attached to the

Russian Armies, has made a special study of the question in his book.

On 4th June there were thirteen cavalry divisions on Brusilov's front, a sufficiently large mass to have an enormous effect on a disintegrated army such as the Austrians became.

But apparently no plans were made either by Brusilov or by his armies for its use. Two of the armies used their cavalry to relieve infantry in the trenches so as to concentrate more infantry divisions for the initial attack. Possibly this was necessary in view of the shortage of troops. Brusilov himself, although he had spent sixteen years in the cavalry school at Petrograd, regarded this as the most useful rôle. Brusilov thought there had been only one chance for cavalry and that was on the Stokhod in the second stage in July, when a cavalry corps actually on the spot failed to push forward. Brusilov thought there was far too much cavalry in the Russian Army and advocated reducing the number of cavalry divisions by half. This was probably reasonable, considering the difficulty of feeding the fifty odd cavalry divisions on inferior lines of communication.

On the other hand, Kaledin, commanding the Eighth Army, was convinced that a cavalry corps on his front would have achieved enormous results after the 4th June. The Austrian Army was, in his opinion, sufficiently demoralized to fall an easy prey. Unfortunately he had used two of his four cavalry divisions to relieve infantry, Brusilov took one away to the north and his only remaining cavalry division was inadequate on his army front of 120 miles.

THE SOMME

It is difficult to get a true picture of the effects of the Somme Battle on the Germans from the information now available from German sources. This was the last battle which Falkenhayn directed before he was replaced by

Hindenburg and Ludendorff at Supreme Command. It is, therefore, perhaps natural that the picture he paints of the battle should be a very favourable one to the Germans, whereas Ludendorff on taking over takes the usual gloomy view of the incomer in a relief, and considers that everything he has taken over is bad.

The opening of the Somme Battle by an attack on a front of some twenty-five miles north and south of the Somme soon had the effect of stopping the Verdun offensive. The Germans did not expect such a heavy attack from the French south of the Somme and their local command and troops got into a state of some confusion there and withdrew from their second position in front of Biaches contrary to the intentions of Supreme Command.

There were alternative proposals for meeting the attack which was fully expected by the Germans north of the Somme. The first intention of the Supreme Command was to break the British attack by a counter-thrust on a large scale with objectives within the British line. This was, however, rendered impossible by lack of reserves in the west owing to diversion of German troops to Galicia and to the continuance of the Verdun attack, which was considered of more value in wearing out the French Army. The withdrawal of the German line of defence just prior to the attack was the second proposal, but this was vetoed, as it would have involved exchanging first-class defensive positions for other inferior ones, and a mere temporary postponement of the decisive battle.

So the German armies were instructed to hold their positions with such small reserves as were available.

It is interesting to consider what would have been the effect of a withdrawal such as Ludendorff had already carried out in the autumn of 1914 in Poland. With their lack of reserves it would have been folly for the Germans to withdraw unless they had a strong rear position ready. This they had not, nor had they the labour organized at that time to construct it. If they had and had also destroyed roads and railways, it would undoubtedly have delayed the *Entente* offensive till too late in the year to have any great effect. The situation in Russia and Rumania would have been far easier, and the Verdun operation could have continued, possibly up to the capture of Verdun.

At all events there would have been no crisis such as was felt in Germany on Rumania's entry into the war on 27th August.

At this time Falkenhayn was of opinion that the Central Powers could not now win the war by the military destruction of one or more of their enemies by means of a few great concentrated efforts. He had concluded that it was a case of holding out and hammering into the *Entente* that the price of continuing the war and destroying Germany was too great to pay.

At the end of August the Kaiser sent for Hindenburg and Ludendorff for a consultation on the military situation. As this entrenched on the authority of the Chief of General Staff, Falkenhayn resigned, and his resignation was accepted. Hindenburg and Ludendorff were appointed to the Supreme Command.

FALKENHAYN

Col. Bauer describes Falkenhayn as follows :—

" He possessed great merits, and his capacity for work was boundless. He had a good memory and was quick in decision. Take him all round, he was a man of exceptional disposition, and would have made a brilliant statesman, diplomat or parliamentarian, but Commander-in-Chief fitted him least."

In January, 1915, we find Moltke, the fallen Chief of General Staff, writing privately to the Kaiser with whom he had remained on friendly terms, and expressing his opinion rather freely on his successor, Falkenhayn :—

" He (Falkenhayn) is a real danger to the Fatherland

90 GERMAN STRATEGY IN THE GREAT WAR

. . . his strategy is one of lost opportunities. Through his short-sightedness . . . I specially do not say his ambition —we have suffered a severe defeat on the Yser."

These are rather hard words when we remember that Falkenhayn had taken over a losing cause from Moltke in September, 1914.

The actual events leading to Falkenhayn's fall are interesting, as apparently it was brought about by the influence of the Junior Staff at O.H.L., just as Prittwitz's and Moltke's removal had been. We are indebted for these accounts to Col. Bauer, who, according to his own reckoning, must have been somewhat of a " Kingmaker."

The Junior Staff were apparently alarmed at the losses in numbers and morale at Verdun, and on the Somme in August, 1916, and urged Tappen and then Bauer to take some action. After some delay, Bauer approached the War Minister on the subject, but nothing happened. Then he went to Gen. von Plessen (Kaiser's Military Cabinet), who was not at all pleased.

But nothing happened till Rumania declared war, when Bauer again went to Plessen and suggested that only Ludendorff could save the situation. The Kaiser apparently approved of this idea, for Hindenburg and Ludendorff were summoned.

In judging Falkenhayn, we must remember his success as an army commander in the field, for he went to command the Ninth German Army in the Rumanian Campaign on leaving O.H.L. and led it with great success under none too easy conditions. He afterwards went to the Turkish Front to control all the Turkish armies, but he did not save them from defeat in 1918.

Falkenhayn died in 1922.

Ludendorff and the Somme

One of Ludendorff's first acts was to consider the infantry defensive tactics practised by the Germans on the Somme.

"1916" 91

His criticisms were doubtless based on his experiences in the east. He regarded deep dug-outs and cellars in the front line as man-traps and drew attention to the superior value of concrete pill-boxes. He criticized the holding on to front line trenches merely for the sake of holding ground. He also drew attention to the excessive use of the hand grenade in place of the rifle, the value of artillery observation, infantry positions on rear slopes, etc. He came to the conclusion that an improvement in tactics and in equipment (provision of automatic weapons) was necessary.

The *Entente* attacks reached their climax in September and continued throughout October and part of November. During this period the strain on the German troops became very great as there were not sufficient reserves in the west to ensure proper turns in rest. This led to the failure of German divisions at times, especially at Verdun in November and December when the French regained practically all the ground lost earlier in the year. After this the *Entente* offensive of 1916 ceased. The German Front still held.

OBSERVATIONS

Moral factors must be given due weight in making plans in war. Falkenhayn's error in misjudging the strength of the morale of the French Army at Verdun cost the Germans dear.

One of the most important and at the same time most difficult tasks for a commander in modern war is the correct placing of reserves for rapid action on the vast fronts of modern battles. In 1916 the Russians had placed all their reserves on the northern half of their front where they intended to break through, but failed. Consequently they could not exploit Brusilov's success to the full.

CHAPTER XI

THE RUMANIAN CAMPAIGN

Meantime German counter-measures against Rumania had been put into force. The task of concentrating German and Austrian troops for the conquest of Rumania which had been decided on, was very difficult owing to continued pressure on all other fronts. Three divisions sent from the west in the beginning of September, 1916, for the Rumanian Front had to be diverted to the Carpathians. The northern part of the Eastern Front had to be further weakened to replace them.

The plan of operations against Rumania was as follows (Map XIII):

Field-Marshal von Mackensen with Turkish and Bulgarian forces was to invade the Dobrudja and after clearing it was to force a crossing over the Danube and co-operate in an invasion of Wallachia with the army group of the Archduke Charles, the latter consisting of the First Austrian Army on the north and the Ninth German Army, now under Falkenhayn, on the south. These two armies were to concentrate behind the river Maros sufficiently far back to escape interference by the advancing Rumanians who were now invading Transylvania in force.

Now consider the *Entente* strategy in Rumania. The apparent intention was for Russia and Rumania to invade Hungary from the Carpathians and through Transylvania, on a broad front, the advance of the Rumanians assisting to turn the Austrian flank in the Carpathians and open the passes for which the Russians had been fighting so long.

THE RUMANIAN CAMPAIGN

What actually happened was that the Rumanians seized the passes over the Eastern Carpathians into Transylvania practically without fighting.

Their inexperienced army then advanced far too slowly into Transylvania, thus not interfering in the least with the German concentration behind the river Maros. Meanwhile the Russians continued to batter their heads against the strongly held northern passes. In fact, the Rumanian movement did nothing to assist the Russians. Surely the latter should have added strength and speed to the southern turning movement by sending Russian troops through Rumania into Hungary, thus enveloping their enemy by their weak flank instead of continuing costly frontal attacks.

However, the Germans benefited by this. Mackensen at the beginning of September seized Turtukai, Silistria, and Dobric and caused the surrender of nearly two divisions of Rumanians.

At the end of September, Falkenhayn attacked at the Rotenturm Pass, defeated the First Rumanian Army after hard fighting, and gave battle to the Second Rumanian Army near Fogaras and drove them back through the mountains into Rumania as far as Campulung. This caused the Rumanians further north to retreat before the Austrians to the frontier.

The advance then came to a standstill and it was clear that without fresh troops the Rumanians could not be crushed.

German Supreme Command decided to find the troops at any risk and took three divisions and two cavalry divisions from the Commander-in-Chief in the East and a cavalry division from Belgium. This second concentration was completed early in November. The progress of events was then rapid. Mackensen had attacked and driven back the Dobrudja force beyond Constanza on 19th October. He then transferred the bulk of his army to Sistova ready to cross the Danube.

On 11th November, Falkenhayn attacked at the Vulcan

and Szurduk passes; the Rumanians were defeated and driven back to the river Aluta. By the beginning of December the Danube Army, having successfully crossed the river, had joined hands with Falkenhayn west of Bukarest. The remainder of the Ninth Army came through the mountains at the Rotenturm Pass and joined in the advance. Mackensen now took charge of both armies. The Austrians east of Kronstadt took little part in the campaign. By 8th January, when the campaign ended, the Germans had reached the line of the river Danube, Sereth and Trotus. The Russians did not send direct assistance to the Rumanians before the fall of Bukarest. Finally, on the Sereth line, the Russians took a considerable share in the defence.

The wheat and oil resources of Rumania were now at the disposal of Germany, but some of her scanty reserves were tied up in holding the Wallachian Front, as this could not be left entirely to Bulgars, Turks and Austrians.

Ludendorff at first had miscalculated the strength required in the Rumanian Campaign. If the *Entente*, that is, in this case, Russia, had appreciated this in time the final result might have been different. Again, if the Rumanians had devoted themselves to fortifying their mountain frontier efficiently before or directly after their declaration of war, Ludendorff's second combination might not have succeeded.

In this Rumanian Campaign the Germans were on exterior lines with very inferior communications, the railways in Transylvania and Bulgaria being very limited in capacity. The Rumanians and Russians were on interior lines. However, the Germans, by carefully and exactly co-ordinating the movements of their separate forces, defeated the slower moving and apparently slower thinking Rumanians. They did this, too, without any such overwhelming preponderance of force as they had used against Serbia the previous winter. Compare the Germans here on exterior lines with Rennenkampf and Samsonov in 1914. The positions are not dissimilar, but the results are reversed.

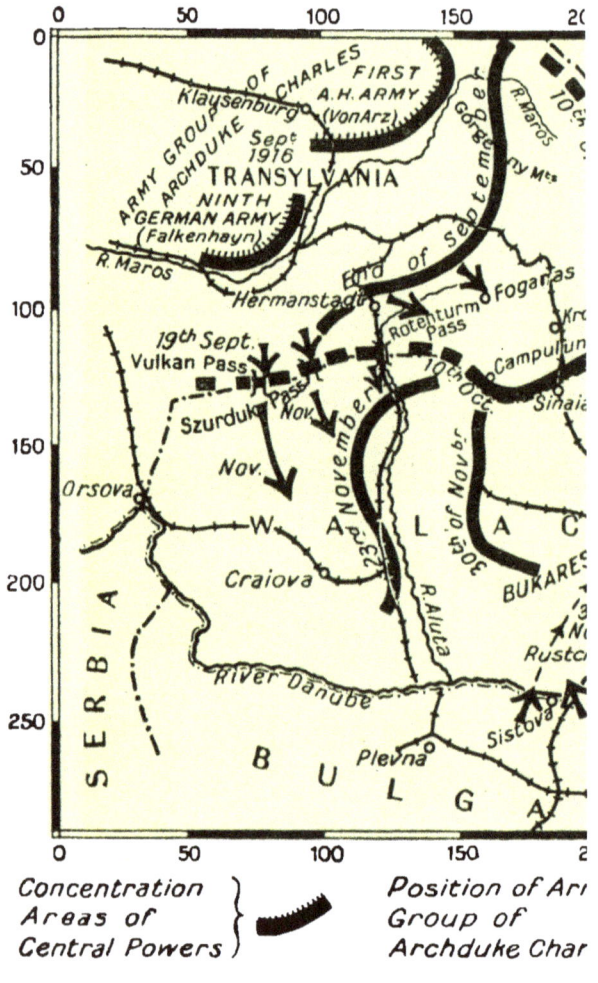

RUMANIAN CA

MAP XIII

THE RUMANIAN CAMPAIGN

OBSERVATIONS

Envelopment will usually produce more rapid and less costly results than frontal attacks on modern defences. The latter should be avoided except in so far as they are necessary to pin down the enemy. Russia persisted in battering at the Carpathians during the Rumanian Campaign instead of turning them by the south.

Co-ordination of the plans of allies is difficult but very necessary. It is especially liable to fail when the enemy has the initiative.

The German campaign in Rumania on exterior lines succeeded in spite of inferior communications. This was due to very careful co-ordination of the moves of the two wings.

It is only fair to the Russians to say that the majority of their generals were very averse to the Rumanians coming into the war at all, they preferred a neutral state on their left flank to a weak ally.

The immediate result of Rumania entering the war was to prolong the Russian Front by 300 miles and to force them to send no less than twenty infantry and seven cavalry divisions into Rumania in $2\frac{1}{2}$ months, a terrible drain on their thinly held front. Moreover, the Rumanian railways were very inferior and badly worked.

The opinion of Brusilov's staff was that the Russians would have captured Lemberg by the end of October if Rumania had not joined in and caused the withdrawal of Russian troops.

However, the Russian attitude to the Rumanians was undoubtedly bad for an ally, for when a protest was made at Russian General Headquarters regarding the smallness of the force sent to Rumania, Alexyiev, the Chief of General Staff, said :—" I have been all along opposed to the intervention of Rumania, but have been forced to agree to it by pressure from France and England. Now that the principle has been accepted, if the Czar ordered me to send fifteen Russian wounded men there, I would not on any account send sixteen."

CHAPTER XII

"1917"

THE *ENTENTE* OFFENSIVE IN THE WEST, 1917. (MAP XV.)

Everything pointed to the Western Front as the scene of desperate fighting in 1917 in which the German armies would be on the defensive. There was also no doubt that simultaneous attacks would be launched in Italy and on the southern part of the Eastern Front, also in the Balkans.

It appeared possible that the *Entente* Powers in the West would not attack until the weather conditions on the Russian Front permitted simultaneous operations.

In this case April was the earliest date. But the situation on the Somme was so tense all the winter that it appeared an attack might start there at any time.

It appeared very probable that wherever the *Entente* attacks were staged their object would be to cut off or reduce the large salient the Germans had pushed into France whose apex was at Roye.

Now a factor which Ludendorff hoped would quickly affect the *Entente* on the west was the unrestricted submarine campaign which opened on 1st February. He therefore desired to postpone the inevitable battles as long as possible. There were other reasons also, rest and training of troops, shortage of ammunition. Further, the German general reserve was inadequate to meet large attacks. It was necessary to increase it by releasing divisions from the line. On the Western Front there were 154 German divisions at this time facing 190 *Entente* divisions and many of the latter were numerically stronger, so it was difficult to thin out the front.

These considerations led to the decision to withdraw from the Gommecort—Peronne—Noyon salient to a previously prepared and very strongly fortified line known to the Germans as the Siegfried line and to the *Entente* as the Hindenburg line which ran from east of Arras—west of Cambrai and St. Quentin to the river Aisne at Vailly. These new defences had actually been commenced the previous September when the Somme battle was at its climax.

In the middle of February the Germans captured a French divisional order in a local attack in the Champagne which clearly indicated a great French offensive on the Aisne in April. This, combined with the preparations observed about Arras, gave the Germans a good idea of the danger points.

The British attack at Arras on 9th April, and the French on the Aisne and east of Rheims on 16th April were checked after severe fighting and after heavy losses on the German side, but definitely checked.

Now the German withdrawal to the Siegfried line in addition to releasing several divisions into reserve, had other effects on these battles.

The intention of General Nivelle had been to attack on a fairly large scale in the neighbourhood of Roye in conjunction with the British attack at Arras. The object being to absorb as much as possible of the German general reserve before the decisive attacks on the Aisne and east of Rheims. These latter attacks were intended to effect a break-through.

The attacks at Roye were ruined by the German withdrawal and although efforts were made to carry them out at St. Quentin after the Germans had been followed up to that point, they failed to draw in any German reserves and were repulsed by the troops in the line. Therefore Nivelle's main attack was carried out with the German reserves more or less untouched and, what is more, those reserves were concentrated at the danger point owing to the

98   GERMAN STRATEGY IN THE GREAT WAR

lack of secrecy and surprise on the part of the *Entente*. Owing to their knowledge of the French plan, the Germans were enabled to concentrate forty divisions in the threatened part of the line to face the attack of forty-eight French divisions.

RUSSIAN REVOLUTION.   (MAP XIV.)

The Russian revolution occurred in March, the Tsar was deposed and a Socialist Government installed. This, of course, had the effect of postponing any proposed Russian offensive, thereby lightening enormously the German burden of defence on all fronts during the critical period of April. It was not till 1st July that attacks planned on a very large scale commenced all along the Russian Front, but principally in the south. Deserters had kept the German Commander-in-Chief in the East well informed of the Russian plans. A German counter-attack on a large scale was planned and six German divisions were transferred from the west for the purpose. The Russian attacks were stopped in spite of considerable success at Kalush (south of Lemberg) and the counter-attack in the direction of Tarnopol was launched on 19th July. It had the effect of breaking up completely the Russian Front south of Brody down to the Rumanian border. The Russian Army, weakened by the revolution, gave way. The remainder of Galicia and Bukovina were cleared of Russians. This *débâcle* showed that Russia had ceased to exist as a military factor in the war.

DEFENCE IN FLANDERS

The British attacks at Messines and Ypres caused very heavy losses to the Germans both in men and material. These combined with French attacks at Verdun in August and the Chemin des Dames in October caused a great strain on the Germans. It almost led to the withdrawal of troops from Russia, but Ludendorff adhered to his plans of finishing Russia off this year. He therefore left sufficient troops

MAP XIV

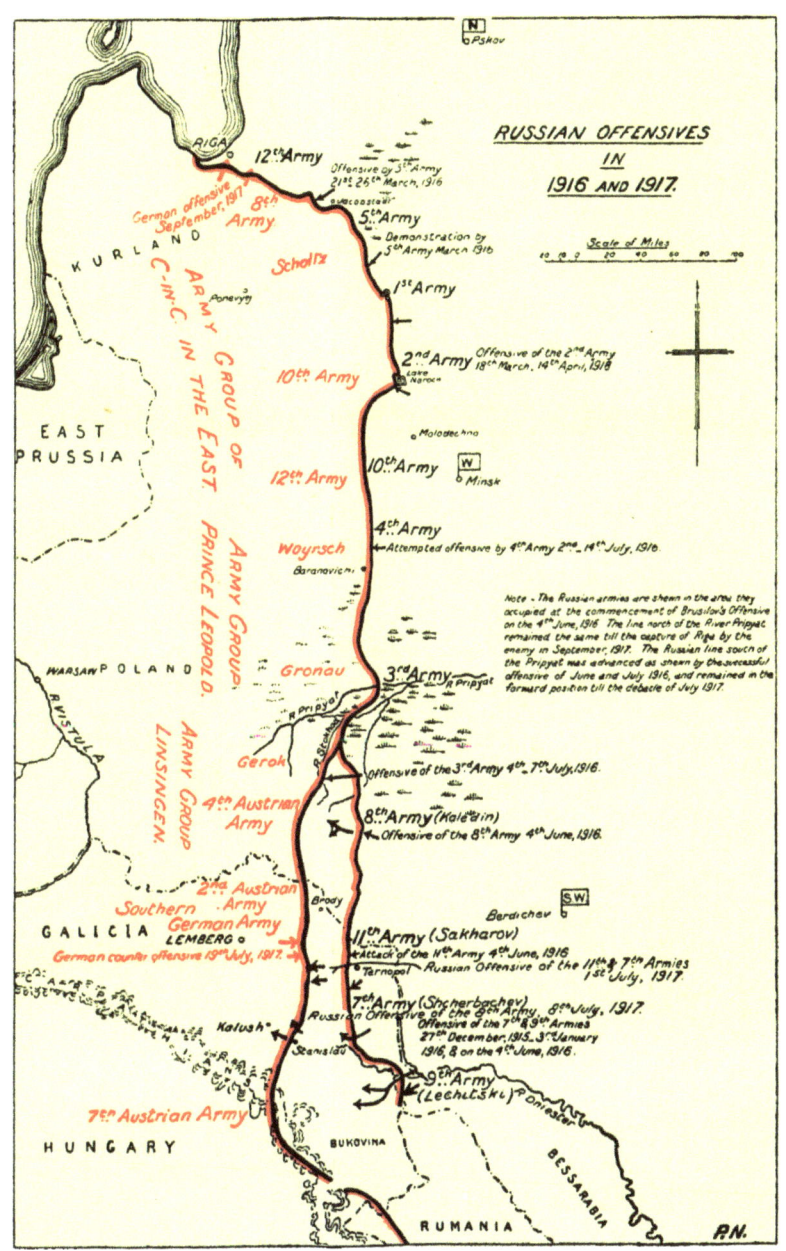

Russian Offensives in 1916 and 1917

there to carry out a series of operations, the attack on Riga, the attack on Osel and Moon Islands, etc.

The chief point of interest was the German development of defensive tactics: first, involving the carefully organized use of counter-attack units and formations, secondly, an increased strength in the front line, but this was soon abandoned in favour of the third development, an advanced zone lightly held in front of their line of resistance. This same idea was developed on the Br'tish side in 1918 into an outpost zone and a battle position.

THE ITALIAN CAMPAIGN

In September the Austrian Army showed signs of collapse under repeated Italian attacks. It became necessary to reinforce with German troops. The only place they could come from was the Eastern Front and that would involve the abandonment of further proposed attacks there. But further successes at the end of the year were very desirable from the point of view of morale of the German Army after its long and arduous defensive in the west.

For these reasons Ludendorff determined to send German troops to Italy, but not for defence. He intended to make full use of them for as great an offensive as possible.

A combined offensive from the Trentino and the Isonzo was very attractive, in fact an operation intended to cut the Italian communications by an attack on two fronts like the crushing of Serbia and Rumania was what Ludendorff would have liked. But the troops were not available this time. Only six to eight German divisions were available, and the Austrians were all very exhausted. So an attack at the weakest point of the Isonzo Front only was decided on.

The attack took place on 24th October and was a complete success, the Germans, under Otto von Below, acting as usual as the spearhead of the attacking armies. The Italians were driven back to the line of the river Piave with great losses in prisoners, guns and stores.

CAMBRAI

From the German point of view the Battle of Cambrai was a complete strategical surprise, and a very unpleasant one. There was nothing to be done but produce reserves to check the British advance. Luckily for the Germans a division on its way from Russia was actually detraining, its leading units having already arrived at Cambrai on 20th November. This division was the decisive factor in localizing the effects of the attack, and its presence was mere luck. By 30th November sufficient troops had been concentrated not only to check the advance, but to counter-attack north and south of the salient that had been created. This counter-attack was successful on the south in breaking into part of the British old line as well as the new.

Ludendorff admits that the fighting at Cambrai gave him valuable hints for a future offensive battle in the west.

OBSERVATIONS

The retreat to the Hindenburg line is an example of a successful strategic withdrawal to a prepared position, upsetting to some extent the enemies' plans and releasing troops for building up a reserve.

Nivelle failed to draw in the hostile reserves before delivering his decisive attack. Also he failed to maintain secrecy or to change his plan when he knew the enemy was aware of it.

Successful deliberate counter-offensives were carried out by the Germans on a large scale both in July, 1917, on the Russian Front and at Cambrai in November, 1917. There were not many instances of such operations during the war. They are difficult to stage rapidly.

Cambrai, the great strategic surprise of position warfare, was very important for its demonstration of the possibilities of tanks properly used.

ENTENTE OFFENSI

MAP XV

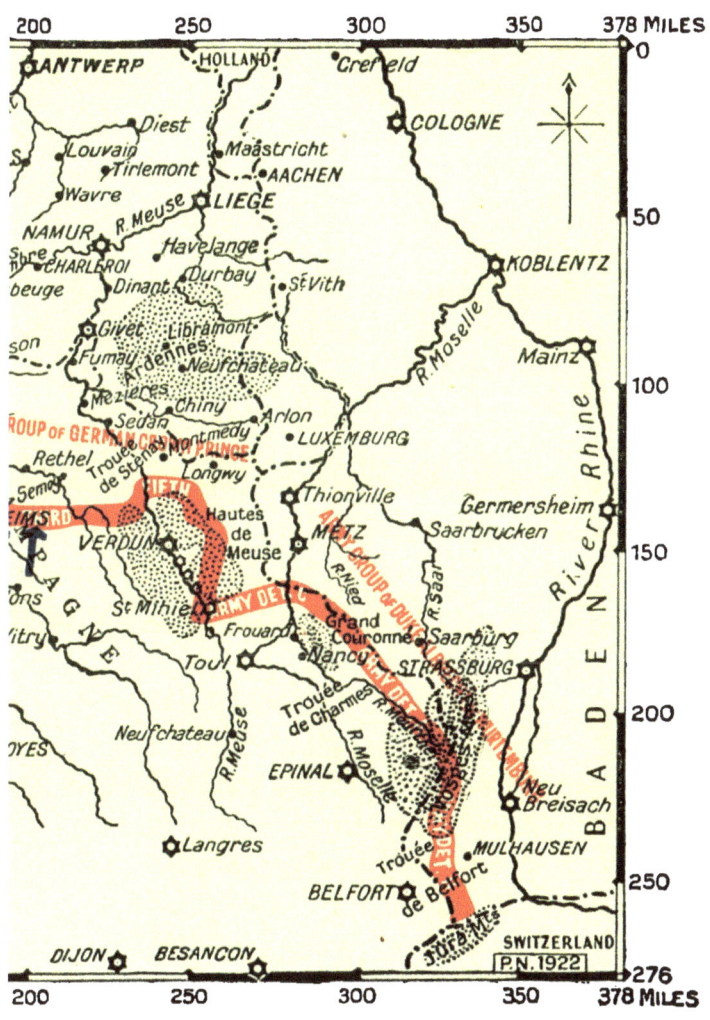

ve, April, 1917

CHAPTER XIII

PREPARATIONS FOR THE OFFENSIVE IN 1918

DECISION TO ATTACK IN THE WEST. (MAP XVI.)

Although peace between Germany and Bolshevik Russia was not signed until 3rd March, 1918, the military situation during the previous winter permitted the wholesale transfer of German troops to the west. In fact, by the end of March, there were barely ten divisions fit for transfer left in the east, and these had all been transferred by the end of April. So that Germany had available early in 1918 the whole of her military resources for use on the Western Front; actually in March, 186 divisions (seventy-eight in reserve). This gave her a military preponderance over the *Entente* which she had not enjoyed since 1914. But this preponderance would certainly be at its maximum early in the year in the spring. The arrival of American troops was a very important factor, and closely bound up with this was the question of submarine warfare. The German Navy was at this time as optimistic as ever regarding the rapid influence of submarine attacks; they considered these would prevent the arrival in decisive numbers of the American Army. German Supreme Command, however, did not accept this opinion blindly and counted on the arrival of American formations beginning in the spring of 1918. But it was considered that they would not in any way compensate the *Entente* for the loss of the Russian Army.

Other factors early in 1918 were the condition of Germany's allies. Austria-Hungary was worn out, the best to be hoped from its army was the holding of its position in Italy.

The Bulgarians had achieved their war aims and only longed for peace. They would remain faithful to Germany only so long as success attended the German Armies. Turkey was faithful but quite exhausted.

Finally it became clear that neither the German Army, still less her allies, would stand the strain of a continued defensive. If the *Entente* got an opportunity of attacking in the west, their enormous material resources, machines and weapons, would enable them to mount attacks on a very broad front, and also aim at surprise as at Cambrai. The morale of the German Army was at this time in no condition to withstand such attacks, quite apart from the great loss in men and material they would inflict. Whereas the troops, inferior though they were to those of 1914, had successfully shown their powers in the attack and in a war of movement as in Italy, Galicia and at Cambrai.

Thus all factors in the situation pointed to an offensive to bring about an early decision. This could not be obtained in Italy or Macedonia. The west was the decisive Front. The offensive is the decisive means of making war. Delay would only serve the *Entente* purpose.

The progress in training the troops for the offensive would enable an attack to be made in the middle of March. Therefore, the decision was made to attack in the west in March.

Locality of the Attack

After a consideration of the forces available, especially the artillery, Ludendorff concluded that he could attack in maximum strength along a continuous front of over 30 miles, utilizing fifty to sixty divisions. He then considered three possible sectors. Flanders between Ypres and Lens, between Arras and St. Quentin or La Fère, and finally both sides of Verdun, pinching out the actual fortress.

Considerations of weather and ground were against Flanders at any rate for an attack early in the year. At Verdun the attack would lead into difficult hilly country.

At Arras—La Fère the country was very suitable except that the old cratered Somme battlefield would have to be crossed.

The *Entente* were holding their Front in great strength about Ypres and Arras, also at Verdun. The weakest portion was on both sides of St. Quentin.

Therefore, from tactical considerations, the centre sector about St. Quentin was the most favourable. Here the attack would strike the enemies' weakest point, the ground was favourable and feasible at any season.

From the strategic point of view, the centre attack offered the most far-reaching results, but only if successful in penetrating to a great depth. The British Army might be separated from the French and crowded into the sea if the attack reached the neighbourhood of the coast via Peronne —Albert—Abbeville. The capture of Amiens alone would create great difficulties for the *Entente* in communications.

The northern attack had strategic objectives of very great importance, that is, the Channel Ports, Dunkirk, Calais, Boulogne, but the results would not be so decisive.

The Verdun attack might lead to a shortening of the Front, but would only produce tactical results. Ludendorff decided to attack in the centre of the three selected sectors, that is, Arras—La Fère. He was influenced by considerations of time, that is, the possibility of an attack early in the season, before the arrival of the Americans, and by tactical considerations, chiefly the weakness of the enemy.

Ludendorff lays more stress on the question of successful tactics than on the strategic objects to be achieved. He quite rightly says that a strategic plan which ignores the tactical factor will fail, and that strategical objectives cannot be reached unless a tactical success is possible. It is interesting to recall the winter battle in Masuria where Ludendorff's plan achieved an immense tactical success, but failed strategically, as Falkenhayn foretold. On the other side of the picture, consider Nivelle's far-reaching

104 GERMAN STRATEGY IN THE GREAT WAR

strategic objectives in April, 1917, which he never came near achieving owing to tactical failure on the Chemin des Dames. It is therefore clear that both strategical and tactical success are essential for the overthrow of the enemy. In open warfare the strategical plan has to be made before the tactical issue arises. In position warfare a tactical success, that is, a rupture of the front, is necessary first.

German Tactics in 1918

A brief summary of the tactical principles laid down by Ludendorff early in 1918 before the German offensive will be of interest.

He insisted on the reduction of losses in the attack by up-to-date tactical training in group tactics (British section), allotting sufficiently wide frontages to enforce a thin assaulting line, and emphasizing the necessity for the use of infantry weapons, that is, the avoidance of mere dependence on an artillery barrage. He insisted that the light machine-gun is the most important infantry weapon and must not be regarded as an auxiliary weapon, it is an integral part of the infantry group. At the same time, the rifleman must be trained to shoot as well.

The heavy machine-gun, light trench mortar, and infantry gun were all auxiliary arms to assist the advance of the infantry in the later stages of the attack when the limit of the artillery barrage was reached or when some strong point held them up. Batteries of infantry guns were being formed, but until they were ready, field guns were to be definitely attached to the battalions, etc., as infantry guns.

Ludendorff considered the battalion to be the tactical unit of the division and the group the tactical unit within the battalion, and his aim was apparently to make each as self-supporting in battle as possible.

Artillery support was to be given in the attack on a scale of twenty to thirty batteries per kilometre, an average of one gun (all natures) per 11 yards.

In the attack in a war of movement the capture of high ground would bring about the tactical decision, and its possession was to be fought for as a matter of principle. This did not by any means involve attacking high ground frontally. We know the German tactics of penetration up the valleys.

CHAPTER XIV

THE FIVE GERMAN OFFENSIVES IN 1918

THE FIRST ATTACK, ARRAS—LA FÈRE. (MAP XVII.) The actual front of attack on 21st March was from Croisilles to Boursies, a distance of 10 miles, and from Gouzeaucourt to Moy on river Oise, a distance of 25 miles, with a gap between of some 9 miles, the Flesquières salient, which was not attacked; in addition, a subsidiary attack, not in such strength as the others, was made on the 8 miles front between Moy and La Fère. The total front involved was some 54 miles on which a total of sixty-four divisions attacked on the first day.

Three German armies attacked and Ludendorff's intention was that the two northern ones, Seventeenth (Otto von Below) and Second (Von der Marwitz) should carry out the decisive attack, protected on their southern flank by Eighteenth Army (Von Hutier). Up to about 6th March, Ludendorff's intention was that the Somme and the Crozat Canal should be the limit of advance for the Eighteenth Army. The Seventeenth Army had the greatest density of attacking troops. The two northern armies were in Ruppecht's army group and the southern one in the Crown Prince's army group. This involving of two army groups in the battle was intentional on Ludendorff's part in order that Supreme Command, that is Ludendorff, might be able to exert a large influence on the tactical conduct of the battle, and also so that in case of success one army group would be free to carry on operations against the British Army, and one against the French Army.

THE FIVE OFFENSIVES IN 1918

The German attack was very successful on the south where the defences were weakest and the British troops thinnest on the ground. In addition, the subsidiary attack between Moy and La Fère came as a surprise and had great success.

Their northern attack (Seventeenth Army) was not so successful as was hoped, the failure to cut off the Flesquières salient is put down to this. Ludendorff states that the Seventeenth Army was not commanded with sufficient energy and that too much latitude was given to the corps. Also that their troops attacked in too dense formation.

Owing to this failure the strategical objective of making for the coast via Peronne—Albert—Abbeville was changed. The weight of the attack was shifted south to the Second and Eighteenth Armies with Amiens as their objective. This, of course, they failed to reach.

It is interesting to follow the changes which took place in the German plan as exemplified by the conduct of the operations by Supreme Command. Although Ludendorff ignores the strategic failure of the Germans, there is no doubt that it was a strategic failure. O.H.L. appreciations and orders before the battle indicate that the main object was to split the French and British by reaching the coast, and to defeat finally the British Army. The French were to be held off south of the Somme by the Eighteenth German Army, who originally were given the rôle of forming a defensive flank from Peronne along the Somme and Crozat Canal. On 6th March Ludendorff appears to have concluded from tactical considerations, that a further offensive against the British north of Peronne would be on too narrow a front, and on that date the Crown Prince's group was told that they would be required to push beyond this river line, but still with the object of meeting and holding the French reserves. The task allotted to Rupprecht's army group was the chief one, and Rupprecht's plan was :—first, to pinch out the Cambrai salient; second, for the Second Army to advance on Peronne and Albert while the Seventeenth Army was to advance north-west on Arras with its left flank on the line Ytres—Bapaume. Rupprecht lays great stress on this latter move being the centre of gravity of the attack of his whole army group. Once the British flank was rolled up to the north, Rupprecht's two offensive armies (Seventeenth and Second) were to move west on Abbeville and the coast.

Now to turn to the actual events. As early as the evening of 21st March, Ludendorff began to move some seven or eight divisions of the German General Reserve not to the front where the strategic objective lay, between Peronne and Bapaume, but down south to the Eighteenth Army front where the tactical soft spot had been found. And on 23rd March, O.H.L. orders definitely point to a change of the axis of the attack to the south, south of the Somme and south of Amiens. On 26th and 27th March, O.H.L. orders indicate a desire to achieve the original objective, but by a very different tactical operation. For orders were issued for a previously prepared operation against Arras to take place on 28th March and at the same time attacks by weak forces against the Third British Army, O.H.L. thinking that the British were nearly done for, while the bulk of the German forces were to turn south, defeat the French, seize Amiens from the south and then turn and roll up the British line. This involved meeting and defeating all the French reserves, in fact Supreme Command intended to tackle both British and French Armies and defeat them in one operation, a very different conception to the original plan.

Now the question arises, was Ludendorff led away by an easy tactical success in the south to ignore one of the principles of war, the maintenance of the objective ? Or, on the other hand, was he right to exploit tactical success although this led his armies against the intact French reserves ? Could the Germans have achieved their strategical aim if they had continued battering with larger forces against the

THE FIVE OFFENSIVES IN 1918

Third British Army ? Or, finally, must we regard the whole operation as a gambler's hazard urged on Supreme Command by the force of circumstances and the knowledge that a passive defence would assuredly lose them the war ?

It is worth considering the prospects of success for a break-through whatever tactical plan the Germans adopted. At this time the *Entente* had nearly sixty divisions in reserve and had also extremely good road and rail communications on the Western Front. Therefore, however successful the German stratagems to conceal the site of their attack, it was almost certain that the *Entente* reserves could reach the battlefield in time to prevent a break-through.

It would appear that the Germans might have been better advised to have absorbed as many of the *Entente* reserves as possible by preliminary battles, involving less expenditure of force on their part, and to have reserved their greatest efforts for a later battle in which a complete break-through might have been possible. All the lessons of the war pointed to the impossibility of a break-through on the Western Front so long as the enemies' reserves were intact. But of course the Germans were fighting against time.

The first great strategical lesson of this operation is the use of surprise and deception by the Germans. By means of preparations and bluff concentrations of troops at various parts of the Western Front, notably between Ypres and Lens, each side of Rheims, round Verdun, and also right in the south, it was hoped to deceive the *Entente* as to the decisive front. These deceptions were very successful. Extraordinary precautions were taken by the Germans in concentrating their troops for the battle and the Germans undoubtedly achieved a strategic surprise although the approximate front of attack and the date were both known to the British before the battle.

The *Entente* as a whole completely failed to concentrate their armies on the battlefield at the decisive time and place.

The British had a very extended front to hold and were forced to safeguard the Channel Ports and the French coal-fields; they therefore had to keep sufficient forces in the north. Actually half the British reserves, i.e. nine out of eighteen divisions, were north of Arras clear of the battle-front. The French on 21st March had the bulk of their reserves in the Verdun area ready to meet an expected attack there or at Rheims or in Lorraine. Of the thirty-nine French divisions in reserve thirty were east of Rheims. Compare the successful German concentration against Nivelle in April, 1917.

British General Headquarters, although well informed by their Intelligence as to the locality and date of the attack, had misconceived the type of attack and fully expected ample time for the assembly of their reserves on the battle-front. This time they never got and the reserves were perforce thrown in piecemeal to plug up gaps in the front.

THE LYS BATTLE. (MAP XVI.)

The Germans broke off the battle in front of Amiens when the *Entente* resistance hardened early in April. Ludendorff then determined to attack in the plain of river Lys, where preparations were complete and where the front was now held very weakly. The attack was carried out on 9th April, in the first instance by trench divisions, that is, divisions holding the line as opposed to assault divisions, and its object was merely to retain the initiative and exhaust the *Entente*. The initial success led the Germans to hope for great and decisive results and they put a considerable proportion of their available reserves into the battle. They did not succeed in achieving any far-reaching success, although the battle did draw in a number of the French divisions and also drew some of the French reserves to the north. It is notable that the salient created by the Germans in the plain of the Lys became just such a slaughter-house

THE FIVE OFFENSIVES IN 1918

for the attackers as Falkenhayn criticized in his appreciation of the unsuccessful break-through attacks by the *Entente* in 1915.

This battle was broken off by the Germans at the end of April.

So far the German efforts had been aimed exclusively at the British Army.

SITUATION AT THE END OF APRIL

At the end of April the Germans had 208 divisions on the Western Front; of these 154 were tired divisions, i.e. had been employed in the battles of March and April, and had not yet recovered, and twenty were 2nd Class divisions, unfit for an offensive. A total of seventy-seven, only twelve fresh, were now in reserve mostly between Amiens and the sea.

At this time the *Entente* had 172 divisions, not counting eight British and two Portuguese more or less broken up. They consisted of fifty-four British, 106 French, four American, six Belgian, and two Italian; besides these, there were numbers of Americans undergoing training. The *Entente* had fifteen British and forty-one French divisions in reserve. Practically the whole of the British Army, but only one-quarter of the French Army had been in the battles. The British reserves were principally between Arras and Ypres, and the French between Compiègne and Doullens.

The problem before the German Supreme Command was where to attack next; there was no question that they must attack to keep the initiative and still try and get a decision.

Where was the strategical danger-point for the *Entente* ? Could a tactical success be gained there ?

Ludendorff considered the Ypres Front, the Somme Front, Chemin des Dames—Rheims, and Montdidier—river Oise, and decided on the Chemin des Dames—Rheims Front. He hoped to absorb enough *Entente* reserves there to be able to return to the attack in Flanders.

Observations

Ludendorff's decision to attack in full strength on the Chemin des Dames must be recognized as wrong if the necessities of the situation are clearly borne in mind.

A rapid and final decision was essential in view of the daily increase in numbers of Americans in France. A mere tactical success, however great, could not end the war. There was no decisive result to be obtained from a breakthrough on the Chemin des Dames, for even a penetration of 30 or 40 miles would not break up the French Armies, the bulk of which were still fresh.

Hitherto all the German efforts had been against the British, surely it would have been best to exploit the exhaustion of one army rather than turn against the fresh army. It may be a matter of opinion which of the *Entente* nations should have been attacked in March, but having started on the British it would be best to go on hammering them.

Again, the only decisive strategic objective within possible reach was the capture of Amiens or even Abbeville which would split the French and British. Therefore, should not Ludendorff have adhered to his original objective however hard its attainment rather than seek after a lightly won but useless success elsewhere.

The Channel ports were also attractive, but their capture alone could not end the war, whereas with the fall of Abbeville, the whole northern coast-line might go too.

If it were necessary to draw off *Entente* reserves from the decisive front, the Amiens area, then a previous subsidiary operation was sound. But it should have had limited forces and limited objectives. The pouring of troops into the salient created on the Marne at the end of May only rendered Foch's ultimate counter-stroke more deadly.

THE FIVE OFFENSIVES IN 1918

ATTACK ON THE CHEMIN DES DAMES, 27TH MAY AND AT NOYON, 9TH JUNE

On 27th May the Germans attacked with twenty-three divisions on a 33-mile front along the Chemin des Dames, and again succeeded in achieving a complete surprise, at any rate a complete strategical surprise, in that there were no *Entente* reserves concentrated to meet the blow. In fact, the *Entente* line was so thinly held that very rapid progress was made and the river Marne was reached from Chateau Thierry eastwards, an advance in depth of 30 miles by the beginning of June.

On 9th June, after the transfer of heavy artillery, an attack by sixteen divisions was launched between Montdidier and Noyon. The *Entente* were prepared and held and counter-attacked the Germans after an advance of some 6 miles.

This was the turn of the tide, the Germans had registered their last success.

An important point in the Marne salient was the railway and supply question for the Germans. All the railways into the salient went by Soissons or by Rheims. The Germans having failed to take Rheims, only had one broadgauge line for the supply of the mass of troops in the salient, a very serious matter, which became a definite danger later.

PLANS FOR THE FINAL ATTACKS AT RHEIMS AND IN FLANDERS

At this time, middle of June, Ludendorff considered that Foch had nearly used up his reserves and that not much more could be expected of the French Army. He was too optimistic.

A fresh offensive was the only thing open to the Germans. The French reserves were mostly on the Montdidier—Compiègne—Chateau Thierry Front. The most favourable operation strategically would be an offensive in Flanders or at the junction of the *Entente* Armies, but there were strong British reserves there, rested and reorganized since the early battles. German documents show that preparations were actually begun for an attack north of the Somme in the direction Doullens—Amiens for the end of June, but this was abandoned and Ludendorff decided to attack again at the weakest point and planned an attack on both sides of Rheims for the middle of July, with one of its objects to improve the communications into the Marne salient. Immediately following this, Ludendorff planned a decisive offensive in Flanders. This was to be the final great effort.

The attacks at Rheims on 15th July were held up by the French before they achieved any success. Their failure was due to lack of surprise. The attacks were mounted exactly like the previous successful German attacks, the preparations were as careful and up to a fairly short time before the date of attack, the *Entente* Front was weakly held. Actually the French knew the sectors and date of the attack and so were able to make very successful arrangements, evacuating the outpost zone east of Rheims and destroying the attackers with their artillery fire. The German commanders and even their troops knew that this great attack had been given away to the French. It is to be supposed that Ludendorff considered he had not the time or freedom of action to delay and change the site, otherwise his adherence to this operation is inconceivable.

ENTENTE COUNTER-STROKE

On 18th July Foch launched his great counter-stroke with the aid of numerous tanks, on the front between Soissons and Chateau Thierry. This attack was very successful in spite of the Germans receiving warning and holding some reserves in readiness. This was the turning-point of the war, the Germans lost the initiative never to regain it.

Owing to the French attack bringing the only broad-gauge railway into the Marne salient under artillery fire on the first

THE FIVE OFFENSIVES IN 1918

day, German supply to the salient was extremely difficult. Further advances by the French on the Soissons flank rendered the salient untenable for this reason, and the Germans were forced to withdraw. Ludendorff complains of the failure of certain German divisions to stand and fight on 15th July and he continues to bemoan failure of morale in some of the German troops from this time on.

But it must be remembered that it was not the troops nor the collapse of morale in Germany that was to blame so much as the action of German Supreme Command in forming two German armies, one to attack and one to hold the line. The Germans frequently boasted of the great deeds of their storm troops. That is very well so long as they had the initiative, but as soon as they lost it, their other army, the passive, ill-trained, ill-cared-for " line holders," were bound to come into action sooner or later against unforeseen *Entente* attacks. Troops will usually behave in accordance with their training and morale. If they have received little training and if they are regarded as second line inferior troops, they will probably behave as such. This the Germans found to their cost and in places their line broke under the repeated *Entente* attacks where they did not expect it to.

The Flanders offensive was abandoned. From now on German strategical plans ceased to exist. Their operations degenerated into attempts to maintain an unbroken front or to conduct an orderly retreat.

There is one important question worth consideration during the fighting of August to November, 1918, and that is the question of the facilities in the way of roads and railways for a German withdrawal.

The Lille—Hirson—Mézières—Metz railway was the great lateral on the German front throughout the war, vital to them for the transfer of reserves. This was cut before the Armistice at Sedan.

The next point is the difficulty of the evacuation of Belgium (both troops and material) through the bottle-neck

116   GERMAN STRATEGY IN THE GREAT WAR

between the Dutch frontier near Liége and, say, Sedan. The difficult country of the Ardennes, poorly provided with railways leading east, lies between. As it was, the Germans at the beginning of the war had to construct a new line through Visé from Aachen so as to enable more traffic to get over the Meuse than Liége could cope with. That traffic was nothing to what there would have been in a forced retreat. Remember the masses of stores abandoned by the Germans in Belgium and also the fact that some of their columns violated the Dutch frontier, when they withdrew after the Armistice.

I think such problems as these must have had their influence on the Germans prior to the Armistice.

OBSERVATIONS ON THE GERMAN OFFENSIVES

Determination to concentrate for the decisive battle is essential to success and a good intelligence service is one of the means of attaining this. A comparison of the *Entente* disposition maps of 21st March and 15th July is very interesting. In the first case we see a thin line of reserves more or less all along the front, rather thinner if anything opposite the front that was actually attacked than elsewhere. On 15th July we see concentrations of reserves in Flanders, the Marne, Rheims and Champagne, east of Champagne not a single division in reserve, and in addition troops were kept available for the great *Entente* counter-stroke.

Surprise is again brought out as one of the chief principles of war. Deceive the opposing commander.

Tactical success and good strategical plans are bound up together. One is no good without the other.

Remember the necessity of economy of force so as to obtain the maximum blow in the decisive attack. Foch succeeded in always keeping a sufficient reserve.

The vital importance of lines of communication is liable to be lost sight of in position warfare. Foch's blow at the

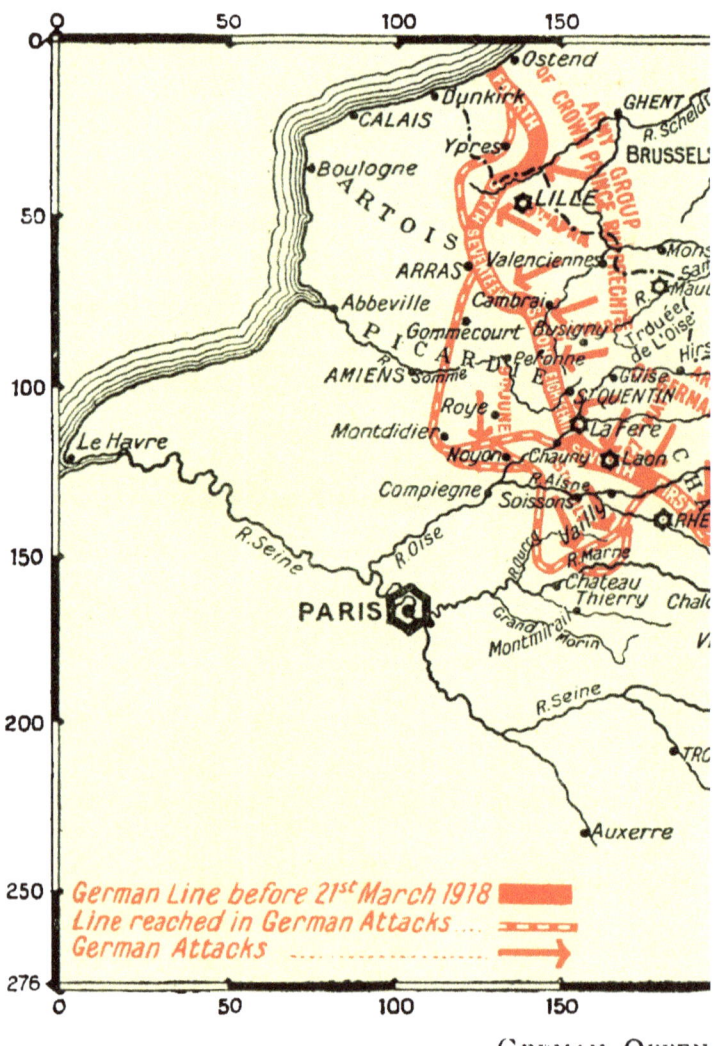

MAP XVI

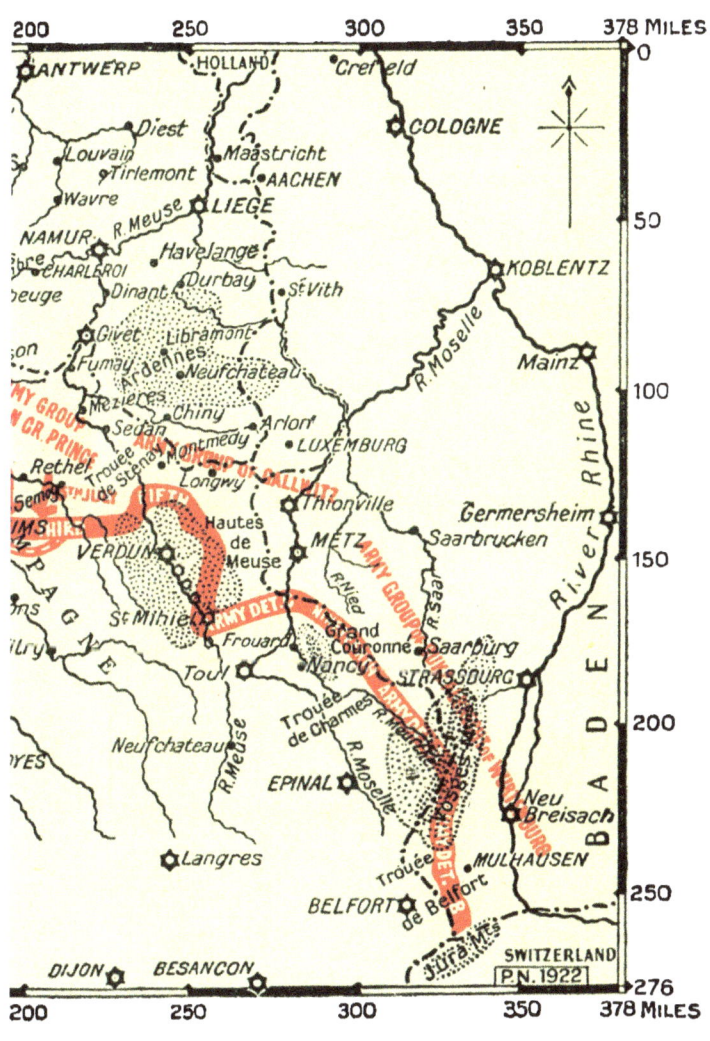

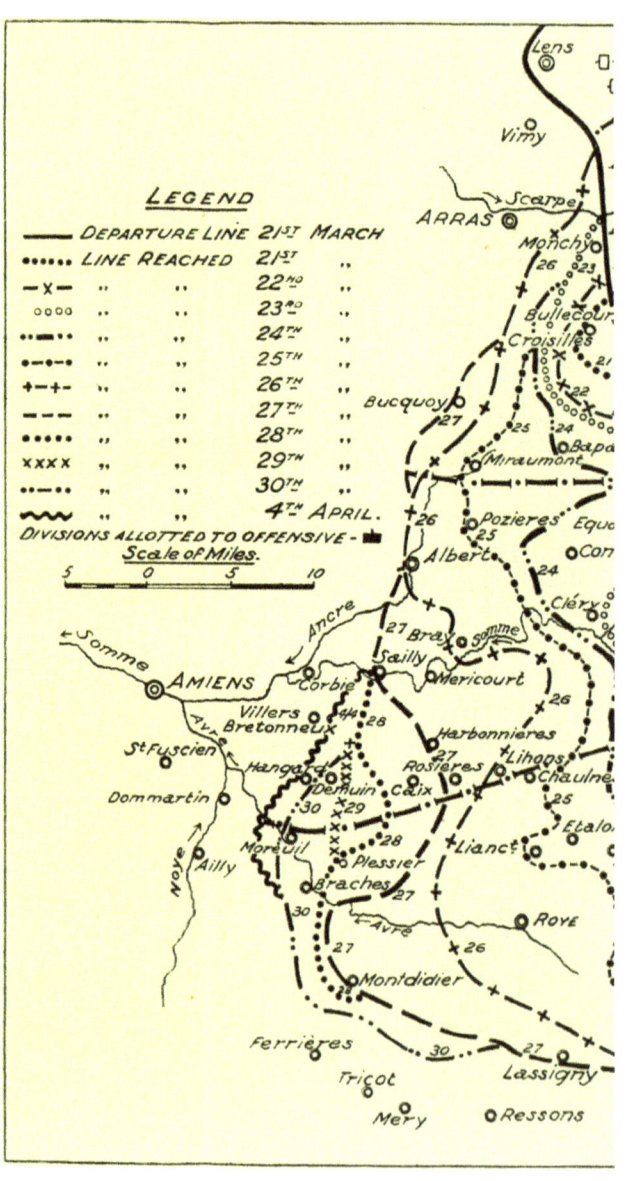

GERMAN ATTACKS, 21ST M

MAP XVII

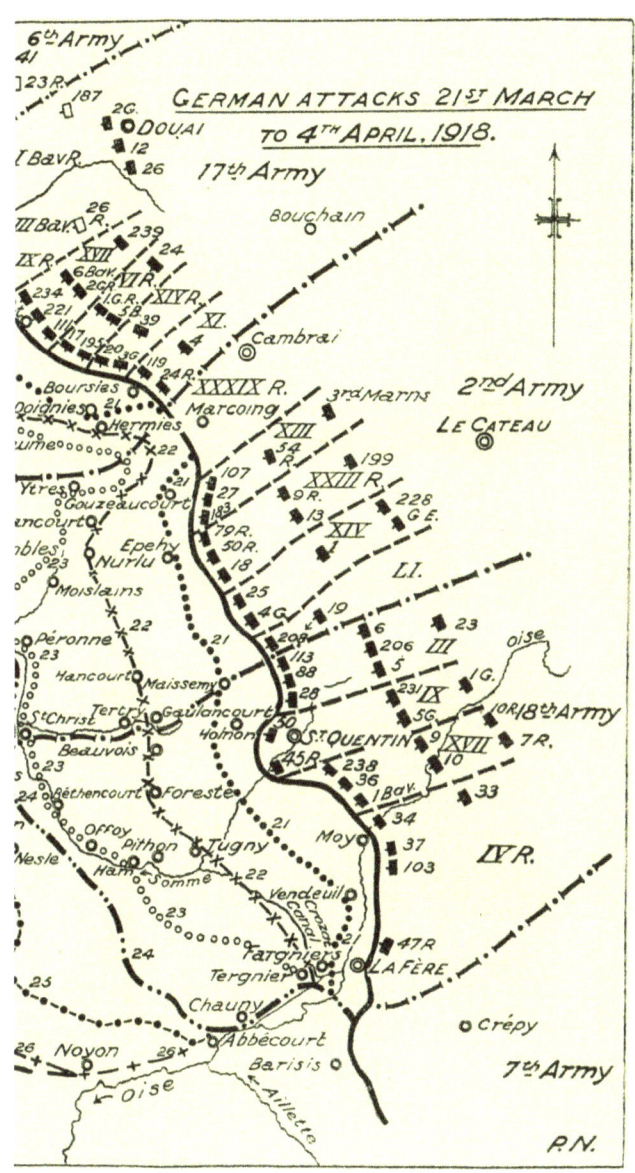

THE FIVE OFFENSIVES IN 1918

lines of communication of the German armies in the Marne salient had decisive results.

It is necessary to keep up-to-date in the means of waging war. Ludendorff utterly failed to appreciate the value of tanks till too late. Tanks were a very decisive factor on the side of the *Entente* in 1918.

CHAPTER XV

LUDENDORFF

Ludendorff's Career

Ludendorff is the greatest military figure that the war produced in the German armies, the only possible rival being perhaps Mackensen who, although holding independent command extraordinarily successfully in Serbia and Rumania, was never opposed by highly-trained and equipped enemies, and was never faced by the same military problems that Ludendorff went so near to solving.

It is necessary to appreciate Ludendorff's position at German Supreme Command. In name he was only " First Quarter-Master General," equivalent to Deputy Chief of the General Staff, in fact it must be recognized that for the last two years and two months of the war he was the Commander-in-Chief of the German Armies, that is to say, of the largest national army the world has ever seen, and, moreover, up to June, 1918, he was a most successful commander.

To appreciate the fact that it was Ludendorff and not Hindenburg who commanded, it is only necessary to remark that whenever Ludendorff was absent from Supreme Command on leave or in his train visiting armies, he was connected by telephone to all army groups. In fact, where Ludendorff moved, there was Supreme Command.

His position *vis-à-vis* Hindenburg may be compared in some measure to that of Gneisenau with Blücher but more exactly to that of the great Moltke in his relations to the Emperor William I in 1866 and 1870.

LUDENDORFF

Erich Ludendorff was born in the province of Posen in 1865, so he was for the Germans a very young general. He received a commission in the infantry in 1882 at the age of seventeen and served with infantry, marines and grenadiers. He passed through the German War College and joined the General Staff as captain in 1895, since when he served almost continuously as a staff officer, first on divisional and corps staffs, then as teacher of tactics at the War College, and finally he joined the inner circle of the Great General Staff at Berlin. Here he became head of the operations section and responsible for the plan of concentration and initial deployment of the German armies for war. It is interesting to note that in 1911–12 Ludendorff urged the formation of three new army corps on a permanent active basis, for he considered them essential to the German plan. The Government and the Reichstag would not agree to this and on Ludendorff commencing a campaign to urge their formation, he was ejected from the Great General Staff and sent to command a regiment. In April, 1914, he became a major-general (at the age of forty-nine) and was given command of an infantry brigade at Strassburg.

On the outbreak of war, Ludendorff became deputy-chief of staff of Bülow's Second Army.

In this position he went as liaison officer with Gen. Von Emmich who was charged with the capture of Liége.

The German plan of attack was to pass several brigades of infantry between the forts by night to converge on and to seize the bridges and citadel while cavalry crossed the Meuse north of the fortress and co-operated against the western face.

The cavalry were checked and the infantry advance went badly. Ludendorff followed one of the infantry brigades in order to be able to report progress. The brigadier was killed and the brigade halted, everything was in confusion. The column was involved in close country between rows of cottages and lanes north of Fort Fleron.

Ludendorff on his own responsibility moved to the front, took command of the column and successfully fought his way by night to the heights overlooking the Meuse bridges and the city. In the morning the morale of his leading companies began to waver. Ludendorff at once ordered an advance to seize the bridges and thinking he saw the white flag flying over the citadel, motored there alone and discovered his mistake; he then summoned the garrison to surrender, which they did, several hundreds of them.

Later on supporting brigades were moved in and the whole city held.

Towards the end of August, Ludendorff was transferred to the Eastern Front to save the situation in East Prussia and here he became Chief of Staff to Hindenburg and the Eighth Army.

From this point on his fortunes lay first on the Eastern Front and his success may be traced by the German victories there, and from September, 1916, at Supreme Command until his fall in October, 1918.

LUDENDORFF'S CHARACTER

Although Ludendorff thought deeply on tactical problems and produced many original tactical ideas, it is not fair to class him merely as a great tactician and no strategist. He has been thus described probably owing to his decisions during the German offensives in 1918. From the nature of the operations in the west in 1917 and 1918 his thoughts may have turned more on tactical problems in those years, but what finer examples of sound and even brilliant strategy can be found than the campaign of Tannenberg and the Masurian Lakes, and the Second Invasion of Poland in 1914. Ludendorff always had large strategical ideas. It appears probable that he makes little mention of strategy in his book in describing the decisions of 1918 owing to those decisions having failed to produce the strategical results desired.

Ludendorff at Supreme Command undoubtedly had a large influence on political matters, he was continually interfering in matters of policy and caused the downfall of more than one Chancellor. His popularity was great in the German Empire, but in the civil government and among the political parties supporting it, his interference was resented.

On one occasion when Ludendorff pressed in vain for Prince Bülow as Chancellor, he remarks:—"Nothing remained but to carry on with my heavy labours and to continue my fight with the Government."

Like most Germans, Ludendorff's judgment of moral factors would appear to have been faulty on occasions. When urging the civil government of Germany to produce more and more men for the front, he disregarded the moral effect on the nation of sending its last manhood to slaughter.

Ludendorff's personal courage, readiness to assume responsibility and driving power are beyond question. He must be a man of great personality and strength of character. He was at all times ready to impose his will on others, for example, Austrian Supreme Command was as clay in his hands even when he was only Chief of Staff of an army group in the east.

On the other hand, he is an egotist of the most pronounced type, making the most of his own achievements and appearing in his book in a vainglorious strain at times. He suffers in this respect by comparison with his great rival Falkenhayn, who, for a German, would appear to have been quite modest.

In spite of such defects Ludendorff worked heart and soul for his country and its cause and used his great brain and character for the service of Germany.

A consideration of the following problem may enable one to form a personal opinion of Ludendorff. If Ludendorff had not been thrown out of the Prussian War Office by the politicians in 1912, he would have been Moltke's Director of

Military Operations at Supreme Command in August, 1914. Knowing that he was an ardent disciple of Schlieffen and his war plan, and knowing also his strength of character, would he have kept Moltke on the right path, and what would have been the result of the Marne Campaign?

APPENDICES

APPENDIX I

NORMAL GERMAN ORGANIZATION IN AUGUST, 1914

1. INFANTRY BRIGADE.
    Headquarters.
    2 Regiments.
    Each Regiment had 3 Battalions and 1 Machine Gun Company (6 guns). Each Battalion had 4 Companies which were numbered from 1 to 12 throughout the Regiment, the Machine Gun Company being numbered 13.

2. ACTIVE DIVISION.
    Headquarters.
    2 Infantry Brigades.
    Divisional Troops.
        1 Field Artillery Brigade of 2 Field Artillery Regiments. Each Field Artillery Regiment, 6 Batteries of 6 guns each. Total, 72 guns.
        1 Pioneer Field Company Engineers.
        1 Divisional Bridging Train.
        1 Divisional Telephone Detachment.
        1 Cavalry Regiment.

3. ACTIVE CORPS.
    Headquarters.
    2 Divisions.
    Corps Troops.
        1 Foot Artillery Battalion, 4 Batteries of 4 guns each.
        1 *Jäger* Battalion.
        1 Pioneer Field Company Engineers.
        Corps Bridging Train.
        Corps Telegraph and Telephone Detachment
        Columns, Trains, etc.

4. CAVALRY DIVISION.
    Headquarters.
    3 Cavalry Brigades.
    Divisional Troops.
        1 Horse Artillery *Abteilung* of 3 Batteries of 4 guns each.
        3 *Jäger* Battalions, each with 6-gun Machine Gun Company.
        1 Machine Gun Battery of 6 guns.
        1 Pioneer Detachment Engineers.
        Heavy and Light Wireless Stations.
        Intelligence Detachment.
        Cavalry Motor Transport Column.
5. CAVALRY BRIGADE.
    Headquarters.
    2 Cavalry Regiments each of 4 Squadrons.
6. FLYING SQUADRON.
    6 Aeroplanes.
    1 Squadron was provided for each Active Corps as well as one for each Army.

STRENGTHS.
Division.   17,500 (12,000 Rifles).
              4,000 Horses (600 Swords).
              24 Machine Guns.
              72 Guns.

Reserve Division as above except that it only had 36 guns.
Corps.   44,000 (25,000 Rifles).
           15,000 Horses (1,200 Swords).
           54 Machine Guns.
           160 Guns.

Reserve Corps same as above except that it only had 88 guns.
Cavalry Division.   7,000 (5,000 Swords and Rifles).
                      5,500 Horses.
                      24 Machine Guns.
                      12 Guns.

In 1914, all Cavalry Divisions did not have 3 *Jäger* Battalions, therefore number of rifles varied.

APPENDIX II
ORDER OF BATTLE OF GERMAN ARMIES, AUGUST, 1914

	Active and Reserve Divisions.	Ersatz Divisions.	Landwehr Brigades.	Cavalry Divisions.
OBERST HEERES LEUTEN (Supreme Command) Chief of General Staff, Von Moltke				
1. FIRST ARMY (Von Kluck) II, III, IV, IX Corps III, IV, IX Reserve Corps 10th, 11th, 27th Landwehr Brigades II Cavalry Corps (Von der Marwitz) TOTAL	14	—	3	3
2. SECOND ARMY (Von Bülow) VII, X, Guard Corps VII, X, Guard Reserve Corps 25th, 29th Landwehr Brigades I Cavalry Corps (Von Richtofen) TOTAL	12	—	2	2
3. THIRD ARMY (Von Hausen) XI, XII (Saxon), XIX (Saxon) Corps XII Reserve Corps 47th Landwehr Brigade TOTAL	8	—	1	—
4. FOURTH ARMY (Duke Albrecht of Würtemberg) VI, VIII, XVIII Corps VIII, XVIII Reserve Corps 49th Landwehr Brigade TOTAL	10	—	1	—
5. FIFTH ARMY (Crown Prince of Prussia) V, XIII, XVI Corps V, VI Reserve Corps, 33rd Reserve Division 13th, 43rd, 45th, 53rd and 9th Bavarian Landwehr Brigades IV Cavalry Corps TOTAL	11	—	5	2
TOTAL for five right wing armies	55		12	7

Equivalent to :—61 divisions and
7 cavalry divisions.

APPENDICES

	Active and Reserve Divisions.	Ersatz Divisions.	Landwehr Brigades.	Cavalry Divisions.
6. SIXTH ARMY (Crown Prince Rupprecht of Bavaria) XXI Corps, I, II, III Bavarian Corps I Bavarian Reserve Corps Guard, 4th, 7th, 8th Ersatz Divisions III Cavalry Corps TOTAL	10	(a) 4	—	3
7. SEVENTH ARMY (Von Heeringen) XIV, XV Corps XIV Reserve Corps, Strassburg Reserve Division Bavarian Ersatz, 19th Ersatz Division 109th, 112th, 114th, 142nd Landwehr Regiments TOTAL	7	(a) 2	2	—
Total for two left wing armies	17	(a) 6	2	3

(a) *Note.*—The six Ersatz Divisions had seventeen Infantry Brigades.

Equivalent to :—27 divisions and
3 cavalry divisions.

TOTAL Western Front	72	6	14	10

Equivalent to :—88 divisions and
10 cavalry divisions.

APPENDICES

	Active and Reserve Divisions.	Landwehr Divisions.	Landwehr Brigades.	Cavalry Divisions.

8. EASTERN FRONT
EIGHTH ARMY (Von Prittwitz)
  I, XVII, XX Corps
  I Reserve Corps, 3rd Reserve Division
  Landwehr Division (Von der Goltz)
  2nd, 6th, 70th Landwehr Brigades
  1st Cavalry Division				

TOTAL	9	1	(b) 3	1

Equivalent to :—11½ divisions and
1 cavalry division.

(b) *Note.*—Main Reserves of Konigsberg, Thorn, Graudenz (Landwehr Brigades), equivalent to at least two more divisions, took part in field operations at an early date.

APPENDIX III

ORDER OF BATTLE OF GERMAN ARMIES AT THE BATTLES OF THE MARNE, VERDUN, NANCY, 6TH SEPTEMBER, 1914

	Divisions.	Infantry Brigades.	Cavalry Divisions.
1. FIRST ARMY II, III, IV, IX Corps IV Reserve Corps II Cavalry Corps TOTAL *Note.*—III Reserve and IX Reserve Corps at Antwerp.	10	—	3
2. SECOND ARMY VII, X, Guard Corps X Reserve Corps I Cavalry Corps TOTAL *Note.*—VII Reserve Corps at Maubeuge. Guard Reserve Corps to Russia.	8	—	2
3. THIRD ARMY XII (Saxon), XIX (Saxon) Corps XII Reserve Corps (less 24th Reserve Division) TOTAL *Note.*—XI Corps to Russia. 24th Reserve Division at Givet.	5	—	—
4. FOURTH ARMY VIII, XVIII Corps VIII, XVIII Reserve Corps 49th Landwehr Brigade TOTAL *Note.*—VI Corps transferred to Fifth Army.	8	1	—
5. FIFTH ARMY V, VI, XIII, XVI Corps V, VI Reserve Corps 33rd Reserve, 2nd Landwehr Divisions 43rd and 45th Landwehr Brigades IV Cavalry Corps TOTAL	14	2	2
TOTAL for five right wing armies	45	3	7

Equivalent to :—46½ divisions and
7 cavalry divisions.
Note.—14½ divisions less than on 18th August.

	Divisions.	Infantry Brigades.	Cavalry Divisions.
6. SIXTH ARMY XXI, II, III Bavarian Corps I Bavarian Reserve Corps 1st Bavarian Landwehr Division Guard, 4th, 8th, 10th Ersatz Divisions 55th Ersatz, 61st Reserve Brigade III Cavalry Corps TOTAL . . . . *Note.*—1st Cavalry Division to Russia.	13	2	2
7. SEVENTH ARMY XIV, XV, I Bavarian, Eberhardt (Ersatz) Corps XIV Reserve Corps 19th Ersatz Division 55th Landwehr Brigade TOTAL	11	1	—
TOTAL for left wing armies . .	24	3	2

Equivalent to :—25½ divisions, and
                2 cavalry divisions.

Note.—A loss of 1½ divisions and 1 cavalry division since 18th August.

APPENDIX IV
RUSSIAN ORGANIZATION

1. INFANTRY REGIMENT.
   Headquarters.
   4 Battalions.
   Machine Gun Section (8 machine guns).
2. INFANTRY DIVISION.
   Headquarters.
   4 Regiments.
   Field Artillery Brigade of 6 8-gun batteries, and Artillery Brigade Park, and other divisional troops.
3. CORPS (normal).
   Headquarters.
   2 Infantry Divisions.
   1 Division Light Howitzers of 2 6-gun batteries, and Howitzer Park.
   1 Battalion Engineers of 3 engineer companies and 2 telegraph companies, and other Corps troops.
4. CAVALRY BRIGADE.
   Headquarters.
   2 Regiments of 6 squadrons each. Strength of a regiment, 1,040 all ranks.
5. CAVALRY DIVISION.
   Headquarters.
   2 Cavalry Brigades.
   Horse Artillery Division of 2 6-gun batteries (field guns).
   A Machine Gun Section of 8 machine guns.
6. CAVALRY CORPS.
   From 2 to 5 Cavalry Divisions.

RUSSIAN ORDER OF BATTLE, AUGUST, 1914

GENERAL HEADQUARTERS. Commander-in-Chief, Grand Duke Nikolas.
Chief of General Staff, General Yanushkevich.
General Quartermaster, General Danilov.

1. NORTH-WEST FRONT. General Jilinski.
   First Army (Rennenkampf).
   III, IV, XX Corps.
   1st, 2nd, Guard Cavalry Divisions.
   1st, 2nd, 3rd Cavalry Divisions.
   Second Army (Samsonov).
   II, VI, XIII, XV, XXIII Corps.
   4th, 6th, 15th Cavalry Divisions.

APPENDICES 131

2. SOUTH-WEST FRONT. General Ivanov.
    Fourth Army (Salza).
    XIV, XVI, III Caucasian, Grenadier Corps.
    13th, 14th Cavalry Divisions.
    Fifth Army (Plehve).
    V, XVII, XIX, XXV Corps.
    7th, 1st Don Cossack Cavalry Divisions.
    Third Army (Ruzski).
    IX, X, XI, XXI Corps.
    9th, 10th, 11th Cavalry Divisions.
    Eighth Army (Brusilov).
    VII, VIII, XII, XXIV Corps.
    12th, 2nd Combined Cossack Cavalry Divisions.
3. INDEPENDENT ARMIES.
    Ninth Army (Lechitski) at Warsaw.
    Guard, I, XVIII Corps.
    Sixth Army at Petrograd.
    Seventh Army at Odessa.
    Army of thé Caucasus.
    I Caucasian. II Turkistan.
4. CORPS FROM DISTANT AREAS *en route* TO THE FRONTS.
    II Caucasian.
    I Turkistan.
    I, II, III, IV, V, Siberian.
    XXII (from Finland).
5. TOTAL STRENGTH OF RUSSIAN ARMY AFTER MOBILIZATION, 1914.
    (i.)   37 Corps containing :—
             70 active infantry divisions.
             35 reserve infantry divisions.
             18 independent rifle brigades.
    (ii.)   36 Cavalry Divisions.
    (iii.)   *Artillery.*
             Infantry Division, 48 field guns each.
             Corps Artillery, 75 batteries, 450 light howitzers.
             Army Artillery, 21 batteries, 84 guns of heavy artillery.
    (iv.)   Aeroplanes 244.
6. TOTAL STRENGTH IN MARCH, 1917, BEFORE THE REVOLUTION.
    (i.)   240 Infantry Divisions.
    (ii.)   54 Cavalry Divisions.
    (iii.)   Aeroplanes 838.

APPENDIX V

LIST OF BOOKS CONSULTED.

	Title.	Author.
English	My War Memories. 2 Vols.	Ludendorff
	General Headquarters, 1914–16, and its Critical Decisions	Falkenhayn
	Duties of the General Staff	Schellendorff
	The March on Paris, 1914	Kluck
	Russia in 1914–17	Gourko
	40 days in 1914	Maurice
	Last Four Months	Maurice
	Sir Douglas Haig's Despatches	Haig
	With the Russian Army, 1914–17. 2 Vols.	Knox
	Ludendorff	Buat
French	Le Grand Etat Major Allemand	Douchy
	Pourquoi l'Allemagne a capitulé	French Gen. Staff
	La Défense de la Position Fortifié d'Anvers en 1914	Lt.-Gen. Deguise
German	Der Fellzug der G. Armee gegen die Rumanen und Russen, 1916–17	Falkenhayn
	Graf Schlieffen und der Weltkrieg	Foerster
	Der Marnefeldzug, 1914	Kuhl
	Mein Bericht zur Marneschlacht	Bülow
	Marnefeldzug	Hausen
	Die Marneschlacht, 1914	Baumgarten Crasius
	Bis Zur Marne	Tappen.
	Antwerpen, 1914	Reichsarchiv
	Die sendung des Oberst-leutnant Hentsch	W. Muller-Loebnitz
	Kurzer strategischer uberblik uber den Weltkrieg, 1914–18	Otto von Moser
	Die Marzoffensive, 1918. Strategie uder taktik	Otto Fehr.
	Der Grosse Krieg in Feld und Heimat	Oberst Bauer
	Schlachten und Gefechte	Great Gen. Staff
	Die Wiederherstellung der Eisenbahnen des Westlichen Kriegsschamplatzes	Kretzchman
	Der Grosse Krieg, Vol. III. Organizationen	Schwarte
	Technik im Weltkrieg	Schwarte
	Articles in R.U.S.I. Journal.	
	,, ,, Army Quarterly.	
	,, ,, R.E. Journal.	
	The Times Literary Supplement.	
	Articles in Revue Militaire General.	
	,, ,, Revue Militaire Swisse.	
	,, ,, Militar-Wochen blatt.	
	Russian Historical Military Review.	

www.ingramcontent.com/pod-product-compliance
Lightning Source LLC
Chambersburg PA
CBHW040301170426
43193CB00021B/2972